PENGUIN BOOKS
George V

Sir David Cannadine is Dodge Professor of History
at Princeton University, Visiting Professor at Oxford
University and the editor of the *National Dictionary
of Biography*. His major works include *The Decline
and Fall of the British Aristocracy*, *Ornamentalism*,
Class in Britain and *Mellon: An American Life*.
He is the general editor of two major series: *The
Penguin History of Britain* and *The Penguin History
of Europe*. *Victorious Century* is his volume in the
former series.

DAVID CANNADINE

George V

The Unexpected King

PENGUIN BOOKS

PENGUIN BOOKS

UK | USA | Canada | Ireland | Australia
India | New Zealand | South Africa

Penguin Books is part of the Penguin Random House group of companies
whose addresses can be found at global.penguinrandomhouse.com.

First published by Allen Lane 2014
First published in Penguin Books 2018
001

Copyright © David Cannadine, 2014

The moral right of the author has been asserted

Set in 9.5/13.5 pt Sabon LT Std
Typeset by Jouve (UK), Milton Keynes
Printed and bound in Great Britain by Clays Ltd, Elcograf S.p.A

ISBN: 978-0-141-98872-6

www.greenpenguin.co.uk

Penguin Random House is committed to a
sustainable future for our business, our readers
and our planet. This book is made from Forest
Stewardship Council® certified paper.

Contents

For Hannah and for Claude

Preface

> No epoch in the life of a nation is exactly outlined by
> a sovereign's reign.
>
> John Buchan, *The King's Grace*[1]

Monarchs have always been by definition multi-tasking
people, and the biography of any sovereign should ideally
give attention to all the many things they do and are. It
should narrate the life of an individual, who is born, brought
up, educated, marries, begets children, celebrates birthdays,
perhaps grows old, and dies. But monarchy is also an institu-
tion, which is temporarily embodied in the person of one
particular sovereign, who in modern times enjoys rights and
bears responsibilities under the law and the constitution, and
who plays a part in government and public affairs ranging all
the way from the dominant to the decorative. Moreover,
crowned heads of state are iconic personages, embodying a
nation's (and, sometimes, an empire's) history, traditions,
identity and sense of itself, which are often articulated
through spectacle and pageantry, of which kings and queens
are the charismatic centre and ceremonial cynosure. Monarchies also project their own images of themselves, via the
media, and in turn images – and imaginings – are projected

back by their peoples and their subjects, who see in their sovereign qualities and attributes that may or may not be real or true. They also function in a broader historical context which they may sometimes help define and even occasionally dictate; but, as John Buchan's words make plain, they do not necessarily do so, and they have not done so in Britain in modern times, when sovereigns reign rather than rule. In writing this brief life of King George V, I have tried to keep these perspectives in view and these considerations and constraints in mind. His years on the throne, from 1910 to 1936, do not mark a period of historic time that could plausibly be called the 'Georgian age'. Yet he was, without question, a multi-tasking monarch, discharging some kingly functions well, but others less so; and as Emperor of India and sovereign of dominions beyond the seas, he was undeniably a global figure. But he had not grown up expecting to inherit the throne or to wear the crown.

A Note on Names

In terms of both the names they were given and the titles they bore, there was a high level of repetition among members of the British royal family across the generations during the second half of the nineteenth century and the first half of the twentieth. Thus Edward VII, George V and Edward VIII were all at one time styled Prince of Wales; George V and George VI were both created Duke of York; Edward VII and George VI were both given Albert as their first name, and as a result, both of them were known in the royal family as 'Bertie'.

Such repetitions, and the frequency with which male members of the royal family also changed their titles, sometimes (as in the case of George V) from prince to duke to prince to king, can cause considerable confusion, and there is no easy solution to this difficulty. I have adopted the same stern convention used by Harold Nicolson in his biography of George V, where he called people by the title they possessed at the time of which he was writing, and I have also, on occasions, used family names where it seemed more appropriate, or in the interests of clarity.

Here are the names and titles of the four kings and their wives who are mentioned in this book:

King Edward VII, eldest son of Queen Victoria and Prince Albert: Prince Albert Edward, subsequently Prince of Wales, Edward VII and Emperor of India. Known in the royal family as 'Bertie' (and, less affectionately in later life, by some of his friends as 'Tum Tum'). His wife, Princess Alexandra of Denmark, was subsequently Princess of Wales and Queen Alexandra and Empress of India, and she was known as 'Alix'.

King George V, eldest surviving son of King Edward VII and Queen Alexandra: Prince George Frederick Ernest Albert, subsequently Duke of York, Duke of Cornwall and York, Prince of Wales, George V and Emperor of India. His wife was christened Victoria Mary, but was always known as 'Princess May', until she became queen and empress, when she reverted to 'Mary'.

King Edward VIII, eldest son of King George V and Queen Mary: Prince Edward Albert Christian George Andrew Patrick David, subsequently Prince of Wales, Edward VIII and Emperor of India, and, after his abdication, Duke of Windsor. He was always known by his family as 'David'. He married Wallis Simpson, who became Duchess of Windsor.

King George VI, second son of King George V and Queen Mary: Prince Albert Frederick Arthur George, subsequently Duke of York, George VI and (until 1947) Emperor of India. Like King Edward VII, he was always known in the royal family as 'Bertie'. His wife was Lady

Elizabeth Bowes-Lyon, subsequently Duchess of York, Queen Elizabeth and (until 1947) Empress of India, and, after her husband's death, Queen Elizabeth the Queen Mother.

The British political party that was in power for most of the life and reign of King George V, either on its own or in coalition, was popularly known as the 'Tory Party' in recognition of its late seventeenth- and eighteenth-century antecedents. In Disraeli's day, its formal title was the 'Conservative Party', and its supporters and MPs were called 'Conservatives'. But after Gladstone introduced Home Rule for Ireland, the party became strongly committed to preserving the union between Great Britain and Ireland, and changed its name to the 'Conservative and Unionist Party', and its supporters and MPs were often called 'Unionists'. Throughout King George's reign, 'Tories', 'Conservatives' and 'Unionists' were essentially the same people, and I have used these three designations interchangeably.

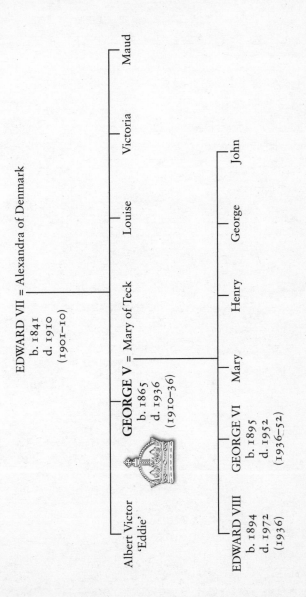

EDWARD VII = Alexandra of Denmark
b. 1841
d. 1910
(1901–10)

Albert Victor
'Eddie'

GEORGE V = Mary of Teck
b. 1865
d. 1936
(1910–36)

Louise   Victoria   Maud

EDWARD VIII
b. 1894
d. 1972
(1936)

GEORGE VI
b. 1895
d. 1952
(1936–52)

Mary   Henry   George   John

George V

There is nothing quite like the status of our Crown in the modern world.

John Buchan, The King's Grace

I
Victorian Grandchild

1865–1901

The nineteenth century began as an era of hope, and till near its close was in Britain an era of confidence.

John Buchan, *The King's Grace*[1]

The future King-Emperor George V, who would reign from 1910 to 1936, was born at Marlborough House, the palatial London residence of his parents, on 3 June 1865, and he would be christened Prince George Frederick Ernest Albert. He was the second son of Albert Edward, Prince of Wales and later King Edward VII, otherwise known as 'Bertie', and of Princess Alexandra, daughter of King Christian IX of Denmark and always called 'Alix'; while his paternal grandmother was the bereaved but intimidating Queen Victoria, then in the twenty-eighth year of her reign and the fourth year of her widowhood since the death of her beloved Prince Albert in 1861. At the time of Prince George's birth, the royal house of the United Kingdom of Great Britain and Ireland was at the apex of the pre-eminent industrial, financial, imperial and maritime nation in the world. Since the final defeat of Napoleon in 1815, Britain had been the foremost great power on the globe, and its exceptional economic success had been proclaimed at the Great Exhibition, held at the Crystal Palace in 1851. It had pioneered industrial manufacturing and railway construction; its bankers and merchants invested in and traded across every continent; millions of Britons were emigrating to the colonies of settlement in Canada, Australia, New Zealand and South Africa; after the rebellion of 1857, India had been drawn into closer association with the British government and crown; and this seaborne empire was held together by shared Britannic sentiment and unchallenged naval supremacy. Here was a country and empire lording it over the present and pioneering the future, for which Thomas Babington Macaulay's best-selling *History of England*, published between 1848 and 1855, furnished an appropriately uplifting version of the national past.

Part cause, part consequence of Britain's remarkable progress, unprecedented prosperity and global pre-eminence was a domestic stability that no other nation could rival. In 1848, much of Europe had been rent by revolutions, and the American Civil War had only ended shortly before Prince George was born. In Britain, by contrast, the franchise had been peacefully extended by the Great Reform Act of 1832, the traumas of the 1840s, including deep economic vicissitudes, Chartist protests and the Irish potato famine, had long since been left behind, and a Second Reform Act would be passed two years after Prince George's birth. Yet mid-Victorian Britain, although unusually stable, was no democracy: fewer than one-tenth of all men (and no women) had the vote; the House of Commons was dominated by the traditional titled and territorial classes; the House of Lords was legislatively supreme in all matters except finance; and the aristocracy, augmented by talented and ambitious outsiders such as Disraeli and Gladstone, still ruled. When Prince George was born, the prime minister was Lord Palmerston, an Anglo-Irish grandee whose experience of government dated back to the early nineteenth century. On his death later that year, Palmerston would be followed by Lord John Russell, a younger son of the Duke of Bedford, and soon after he would be succeeded by the Earl of Derby. In the Britain of the 1860s, the world seemed for the few, and especially for the very few, and at the summit of this layered, ordered social hierarchy, in which virtually everyone knew their place, was the British royal family.

But how British was the regal house into which Prince George had been born, how much of a family was it, and how secure was it at the apex of the social hierarchy? Throughout the eighteenth century, all of Britain's Hanoverian monarchs had married German princesses, and Queen Victoria's father, the Duke of Kent, had followed this custom. In the same way, Victoria wed Prince Albert of Saxe-Coburg-Gotha, an arranged match, promoted by Albert's uncle, who had recently become king of the Belgians, but which soon evolved into one of the great royal romances of modern times. The queen, in turn, sought to marry off her children into European royalty, initially in the case of her eldest daughter, another Victoria, who wed the Crown Prince of Prussia, making her in due course, albeit briefly, Empress of Germany. Then she fixed up her eldest son, Prince Bertie, with Princess Alix, of the Danish royal house; Alix's sister, Marie, married Alexander III, Emperor of Russia, and her brother, William, became King of Greece. Thus understood, British royalty was not so much nationally rooted, but part of a cosmopolitan, continental-wide caste, encompassing the Protestant realms of the Low Countries, Scandinavia and Germany, and also extending to imperial Russia and parts of the Balkans. As a result, the young Prince George was cousin to the future German emperor, Kaiser Wilhelm II, and the future Russian emperor, Tsar Nicholas II. From this perspective, the purpose of intermarried, continental royalty was to take a broad view of affairs, to manage and mitigate national rivalries and to regulate and orchestrate international relations, and to this end, all members of Europe's major ruling houses were expected to speak English, French and German.

As the products of such a trans-national royal world, both Queen Victoria and her eldest son, the future King Edward VII, were at least as much German as they were British: both were at ease in the courts and capitals of Europe; both were fluent in French and German; and both spoke English with a pronounced German accent. But there the similarities between them ended, for their personal relations were neither warm nor close. The Hanoverians had always disagreed across the generations, with the heir to the throne invariably falling out with his father-king, and the same was true of Victoria and Bertie. The queen saw herself as representing a complete break with her profligate and promiscuous Hanoverian uncles, among them George IV and William IV, and she also came to deplore her eldest son, whom, just two years before Prince George was born, she declared to be 'totally totally unfit ... for ever becoming king'.[2] Bertie had rejected the demanding educational scheme that the queen and Prince Albert had devised for him; he gambled, got into debt and enjoyed the 'fast' company of louche aristocrats and plutocrats; his pre-marital affair with Nellie Clifden devastated his parents; and Albert died from an illness contracted after visiting his son in an effort to get him to mend his ways. In 1863, Bertie married the loyal and long-suffering Princess Alix, but he soon embarked on a lifelong sequence of extra-marital affairs. Victoria did not forgive him for (as she saw it) being responsible for Albert's death, and thereafter she never could look on him 'without a shudder'.[3] She refused to let him see state papers or involve him in official business; she fervently hoped he might never succeed her, and she would come close to achieving that objective.

Bertie's idleness, indebtedness and philandering were one reason why the 1860s were a difficult decade for the British monarchy; but nor was Queen Victoria's own conduct as sovereign entirely above reproach. After Prince Albert's death, she had effectively withdrawn from public life, refusing to open Parliament in state, giving up visits to the great provincial cities, no longer living at Buckingham Palace and spending her time secluded at Windsor, Osborne or Balmoral. And although she continued to receive her ministers, and to scrutinize state papers, her increasingly eccentric and reclusive behaviour led many in London's social and political circles to fear that, like her grandfather King George III, she was becoming insane. Shortly after Prince

George was born, the journalist Walter Bagehot published a book entitled *The English Constitution*, in which he memorably described the queen and the Prince of Wales as 'a retired widow and an unemployed youth', and the phrase struck home.[4] By the end of the 1860s, there would be demands for the monarchy's abolition, on the grounds that it was doing so little it might as well be done away with altogether and be replaced by a republic (as would happen in France in 1870). Meanwhile, Bagehot was unclear just what powers, as a 'constitutional monarchy', the British crown in fact exerted. In one famous passage, he noted that the sovereign had only three rights: to be consulted, to encourage and to warn. But he also conceded that the crown did more than it seemed to do, and that Prince Albert had gained and wielded 'great power'.[5] So, indeed, he had; and although, to her great regret, she was less influential during the later decades of her reign, Victoria never conceded that the sovereign's rights and prerogatives were as limited as Bagehot averred, and she once declared she would never be queen of 'a democratic monarchy'.[6]

Despite Britain's wide-ranging pre-eminence, its reigning royal house into which Prince George was born was thus more immigrant than indigenous, and it was also neither a wholly happy family nor a wholly comfortable dynasty. Moreover, there was serious concern about the succession: for not only did Bertie seem completely unsuited to the task of monarchy, but his firstborn son, Prince Albert Victor Christian Edward (known as 'Eddy'), was even more of a problem, as it soon became clear that he was quiet, delicate, lethargic, apathetic and a slow developer (he may, indeed, have suffered from what would now be termed attention deficit disorder). Although eighteen months older than Prince George, Prince Eddy would always depend on his younger and more reliable brother. But despite Eddy's shortcomings, it seemed inevitable he would one day inherit the throne, and this in turn meant that, as the younger son, Prince George lived the first *twenty-six* years of his life with no expectation of ever becoming king: like many monarchs whose reigns later turned out well, he was not born to succeed. The inter-generational tensions in the royal family also continued, for there had been disagreements between Prince George's parents and his grandmother as to what the new arrival should be called. The Prince and Princess of Wales had long settled on 'George Frederick', but the queen did not like 'George' because it was too Hanoverian, and although she preferred 'Frederick', she also wanted him, like all her male descendants, to be called 'Albert'. Prince George's parents reluctantly agreed (adding 'Ernest', another Hanoverian name, for good measure), but they stood by their original choice: 'they are the names we like, and have decided on for some time,' the Prince of Wales defiantly told his mother.[7]

Such was the world in which Prince George grew up, and the royal nursery would soon be enlarged by the arrival of his sisters, Princesses Louise, Victoria and Maud, between 1867 and 1869 (a third son, Prince Alexander, born in 1871, died within hours of his birth). In some ways, Prince George enjoyed a much happier childhood than his father had endured. For unlike Prince Albert, and despite volcanic flashes of Hanoverian temper, the Prince of Wales was no domestic tyrant but an affectionate and demonstrative parent, who indulged rather than intimidated his children. Moreover, the Princess of Wales insisted her boys and girls should be brought up simply, as she had been in Denmark, and at Sandringham, the Norfolk estate which Bertie had acquired three years before Prince George's birth, they were liberated from the formality of court life, enjoying boisterous practical jokes and noisy knockabout games. Queen Victoria approved of the 'great simplicity and absence of all pride' in her grandchildren, but she also complained that her daughter-in-law spoiled them: 'they are such ill-bred, ill-trained children,' she lamented. 'I can't fancy them at all.'[8] The Queen's censure may have been an indication of her grandchildren's freedom and happiness; but Princess Alix was also a cloying, sentimental and suffocating mother, who never wanted her children to grow up: she hoped her daughters would remain single (and subservient), and she would still be penning letters in the language of the nursery to her two sons in their early twenties. When he was a naval officer in command of a gunboat, she would write to Prince George 'with a great big kiss for your lovely little face'. And he, in turn, began his letters to 'My own darling sweet little beloved Motherdear' and signed off 'Your loving little Georgy'.[9]

But while in some ways the Prince and Princess of Wales were devoted, even doting parents, they could also be indifferent to the point of negligence, and this was especially so when it came to overseeing their children's education. Bertie was determined that they should be spared the cruel and inappropriate schooling regimen against which he had rebelled, while Alix's intellect had never developed beyond adolescence, and her self-absorption would increase in later life on account of her chronic deafness. The prince had had too much education, and the princess too little, with the result that both of them doubted it would be of much benefit to their own brood. 'The melancholy thing,' Lady Frederick Cavendish lamented about Bertie and Alix, 'is that neither he nor the darling Princess ever care to open a book', and their children would be equally lacking in a love of learning or intellectual curiosity.[10] Like many upper-class girls, Princesses Louise, Victoria and Maud received virtually no education, and as adults they would scarcely be able to read and write; while Princes Eddy and George fared little better. In 1871, when they were aged seven and six, their schooling was entrusted to the Reverend John Dalton, a thirty-two-year-old curate, whose only qualification was his connection with the parish of Whippingham, near Osborne, where he had come to Queen Victoria's notice. But Dalton was more interested in strict schoolroom discipline and in ingratiating himself with royalty than in educating the young princes. He was a bad teacher yet a gifted court intriguer, and he early on duped Bertie and Alix into believing that their boys were far from bright, but that he alone might improve them. In fact, he lacked both the inclination and the capacity to do so, and their unquestioning trust of Dalton was a serious parental failure.

The non-results of this non-education were soon apparent. Prince Eddy was lazy, vacant and unable to concentrate; Prince George would always write in a slow, deliberate, childlike hand, and his spelling was permanently insecure; and by the ages of nine and eight, when many young European royals had already mastered it, neither boy could speak or understand French. Dalton's solution to the problems he himself had largely created was to urge that the two princes should be trained as naval cadets and that he should accompany them, and in October 1877 tutor and charges were duly despatched to HMS *Britannia*, a naval training ship anchored in the River Dart in Devon. Prince George made good progress, but Prince Eddy learned nothing and was the despair of those who vainly tried to teach him. Once more, Dalton evaded responsibility for this latest educational debacle, and proposed an even more bizarre way of dealing with it: the two boys should go on an extended sea voyage, and he would again go with them. Accordingly, in September 1879, Dalton and the two princes set sail on HMS *Bacchante*, an ironclad corvette, which would be their principal home during the next three years. To isolate the future King of England and his only brother on the same ship for so long was an ill-judged and high-risk educational experiment: on several occasions, the *Bacchante* encountered severe weather hundreds of miles from shore, and in the Indian Ocean it was disabled by a storm, drifting helplessly for three days and nights. In 1886, Dalton would publish an account of these royal voyages that exaggerated the princes' attainments, thereby concealing their shortcomings as pupils and his as an instructor; but despite his pedagogic and personal limitations, he would become one of Prince George's few lifelong friends.

The journeys on the *Bacchante* provided the young princes with their first extended encounter with many parts of the British Empire, including the West Indies and the Cape of Good Hope, the Antipodes and Hong Kong, Singapore, Ceylon, Egypt and Gibraltar. Indeed, no royal princes had seen so much of it when at such impressionable ages. On their return, Prince George and his brother were sent to Lausanne to improve their French, but in six months they made little progress, and their later attempts to learn German met with no more success. This was a serious royal deficiency, and it helps explain why Prince George would always prefer the empire (which to him was 'home') to Europe (which he disliked and distrusted as 'abroad'). But it may also have been because that phase of his life which overlapped with his grandmother's latter years witnessed a new, unprecedented era in Britain's imperial expansion, consolidation and consciousness: Canada was made a confederation in 1867; Victoria was proclaimed Empress of India a decade later; as Africa was partitioned, Britain obtained the lion's share of the spoils; and in 1900 Australia would become a federation. Of this far-flung maritime imperium, the queen-empress became both cynosure and symbol: her middle-aged unpopularity forgotten, and her widowed seclusion overcome, as she enjoyed late-life veneration and global homage at her Golden and Diamond Jubilees, which were also celebrations of national prosperity and progress, as well as imperial might and world-encompassing dominion. Prince George would always look back on the spectacles of 1887 and 1897 with pride and (increasingly) nostalgia. The empire mattered more to him than to any other British monarch, and he would be the last who would not only live but also die as Emperor of India.

Yet the imperial pride and jingoistic euphoria of the 1880s and 1890s could not entirely conceal growing doubts and fin-de-siècle anxieties about Britain and its empire. By the end of the nineteenth century, the once-unrivalled 'workshop of the world' was losing its competitive edge in industry and manufacture to Germany and the United States, as the mid-Victorian boom turned into the late-Victorian depression. Shortly before the Golden Jubilee of 1887, Home Rule for Ireland became a major political issue, and the Indian National Congress was formed, which would campaign for independence from British imperial dominion; thereafter, the disaffection and agitation in Ireland and in India would lead some to wonder for how long the British Empire could be held together. By the time of the Diamond Jubilee, there were growing concerns as to whether Britain's providential march to European pre-eminence and global greatness could be sustained. Lord Salisbury, the Unionist leader, feared what he called 'disintegration', a sentiment reflected in the most enduring – but disconcerting – work to come out of the celebrations of 1897, Rudyard Kipling's poem 'Recessional', which refused to celebrate glory and success but, instead, dwelt on the ephemerality of earthly dominion and the transience of imperial power. Of more immediate and particular concern was Germany, which had been unified in 1870, five years after Prince George was born. Soon after, the Reich began to mount serious challenges, not only to Britain's economic supremacy, but to also its maritime might; and these were encouraged by Queen Victoria's bombastic and unstable eldest grandson, who became Kaiser Wilhelm II in 1888. On the continent, as in India and Ireland, the prospects were darkening; and throughout King George's reign, much that would happen in the empire and across Europe would cause him worry and woe, disappointment and dismay.

After their linguistic failure in Lausanne, the two princes were separated for the first time: Prince Eddy, still accompanied by Dalton, went to Cambridge, where he fared no better than on *Britannia*, while Prince George resumed the naval career he had effectively begun on the *Bacchante*, where he had been promoted to midshipman. From 1883 until 1891, he alternated between postings afloat (in the North Atlantic, home waters or the Mediterranean) and ashore (at Greenwich and Portsmouth, where he studied subjects such as gunnery and navigation), and in 1889 he received his first independent command. Like many sailors, Prince George embraced a simple Christian faith: he would always be a middle-of-the-road Anglican, and from the time he went to sea, he read the Bible every day. He also began to smoke heavily, and like his father before him, and his second son after him, his health would suffer as a result. Prince George's cloistered upbringing, which his cloying mother had made even more isolating, also meant he had few friends of his own age (his shipmate Charles Cust, who became a lifelong friend and equerry, was a rare exception), while the responsibilities of naval command further inhibited his capacity for empathy or friendship, as well as intensifying the irritability and short temper he had inherited from his father. Like his father, too,

Prince George was obsessed by uniforms and decorations, protocol and etiquette, timing and punctuality; and like many naval officers, he was impatient with nuance and complexity, and he mistrusted imagination and intuition. All his life, he would view the world from the vantage point (and often in the language) of the quarterdeck; in his early twenties, the smile vanished from his face, to be replaced by the bearded stare, by turns intimidating and defiant, baffled and uncomprehending, that scarcely changed thereafter.

By then he may have realized that, while his grandmother was enjoying her earthly apotheosis, neither his father nor his elder brother stood so high in public esteem. The queen-empress had come out of her widowed retirement to widespread popular acclaim, but the Prince of Wales, though no longer youthful, remained unemployed, which meant he continued to gamble and to womanize as he had done since late adolescence, and as a rampant adulterer and unscrupulous sexual predator, he was constantly at risk of catching venereal diseases, or from scandal and blackmail. In 1889, having recently tired of Lady Randolph Churchill, he took up with Daisy Brooke, the future Countess of Warwick. So openly did Bertie flaunt this new relationship that it was too much even for his long-suffering wife; Alix went abroad on a protracted round of family visits to hide her pain and humiliation, and was conspicuously absent from her husband's fiftieth-birthday celebrations. Meanwhile, the prince's finances were reaching a crisis, as his debts mounted, and he was saved, at the eleventh hour, only by the intervention of Lord Rothschild and Baron Hirsch, who made him large loans. Even worse, he was obliged to give evidence in court in the libel action brought by Sir William Gordon Cumming, a member of his circle accused of having cheated at cards during a weekend house party at Tranby Croft, in Yorkshire. Here was a dissolute world of adultery, gambling and fast living utterly at variance with the 'Balmorality' that Victoria and Albert had embodied, and it did not bode well for the future of the monarchy. Prince George remained loyal to his father, dismissing as sanctimonious humbug the public censure to which the Prince of Wales was subjected; but he also resolved to live his own life very differently.

Nor, since he had separated from Prince George, after their abortive French lessons in Lausanne, had Prince Eddy improved. Widely recognized to be charming and sweet-natured, he was his mother's favourite. But he was also gormless and lackadaisical; at Cambridge he showed no aptitude for study – one tutor complained that he scarcely knew the meaning of the words 'to read'; and in conversation he was listless and vague, his sentences trailing off as though he had forgotten what he was going to say.[11] Thereafter, Prince Eddy was commissioned into the 10th Hussars, a fashionable cavalry regiment, but he mastered neither the theory nor the practice of arms, and he was incapable of performing even elementary drill movements on the parade ground. Like many royal men, he was fascinated by uniforms and medals; but unlike his younger brother, it was clear he had no future in a career in the armed services, and his increasingly lax and irresponsible way of life soon became as much the subject of gossip and censure as that of his wayward father. It was rumoured that he was visiting a notorious homosexual brothel in Cleveland Street; he certainly had affairs with women who demanded money in exchange for the return of his letters to them; and he caught gonorrhoea. In 1890, Queen Victoria created Eddy Duke of Clarence and Avondale, and family pressure on him to find 'a good sensible wife with some considerable character' began to mount.[12] But his cousin, Princess Alexandra of Hesse, turned him down, preferring the future Tsar Nicholas II of Russia, and Princess Hélène of Orleans, the daughter of the Count of Paris, pretender to the French throne, was deemed unsuitable because she was a Catholic.

At this point, Bertie and his mother stepped in, insisting that Eddy must marry Princess Victoria Mary of Teck, who was the daughter of Queen Victoria's first cousin, Mary, the Duchess of Teck, and always known as 'May'. Mary's husband, the Duke of Teck, was a descendant of the ruling house of Württemberg in Germany, but his father had made a non-royal, morganatic marriage. This prevented him from succeeding to the throne of Württemberg, and instead the duke and duchess settled in England, where they lived beyond their means and ran up large debts. But Princess May was thought to be 'very well brought up with a good head on her shoulders', she had been much better educated than Prince Eddy or his siblings, she spoke fluent French and German and took a lively interest in the arts.[13] She was also readily available, for no German prince would touch a princess with non-royal blood, and despite his obvious personal failings, there seemed reason to believe she would accept a proposal from Eddy. The prince and princess were duly primed: Eddy was told it was 'for the good of the country', and May was urged to make no 'resistance'.[14] In December 1891, Eddy duly proposed to May during a house party at Luton Hoo, and 'of course' she accepted him. The betrothed pair hardly knew each other, but Eddy's parents and grandmother were delighted, as were the Duke and Duchess of Teck, who would be translated from the fringes of British royalty to the very centre. Yet it was not to be: early in the new year, Eddy caught influenza when out shooting at Sandringham, and on 14 January 1892 he died, just six days after his twenty-eighth birthday. It was neither the first nor the last time that a royal demise would prove to be a blessing, for in his mid-twenties the more stable and reliable Prince George unexpectedly found himself in direct line of succession to the British imperial throne.

At the time of his brother's death, Prince George was recovering from a recent attack of typhoid – the disease which had allegedly killed Prince Albert in 1861, and had almost claimed the life of the Prince of Wales ten years later. But the new heir presumptive, for all his educational and temperamental limitations, was more robust and more responsible than Prince Eddy would ever have been. He reluctantly resigned himself to ending his naval career and made one last, vain attempt to come to terms with German, spending some months with a professor in Heidelberg. To mark his promotion in the royal hierarchy, Prince George was assigned the substantial income that had previously gone to his late brother, he was given his own London accommodation in St James's Palace, along with York Cottage on the Sandringham estate in Norfolk, and the queen

created him Duke of York, Earl of Inverness and Baron Kil-
larney. But the most important requirement of his new
position remained unsatisfied: the duke must marry and
beget children. His own preference was for his cousin, Princess Marie, daughter of the Duke of Edinburgh; but she
refused him. And his mother, Alix, was more possessive
than ever. 'Nothing and nobody can or ever shall come
between me and my darling George boy,' she told him.[15]
But Queen Victoria was in 'a terrible fuss' about her grandson marrying, and she urged him to seek May's hand for
himself.[16] In the shadow of Eddy's death and the wedding
that never was, both young people were shy and diffident,
and they were far from being in love with each other. Nevertheless in the spring of 1893, the Duke of York duly
proposed to Princess May, he was accepted, to widespread
approval and relief, and the wedding took place at the
Chapel Royal, St James's Palace.

Unlike his father, who would shortly be moving on from
Daisy Brooke to Mrs Keppel, the Duke of York would be an
exceptionally loyal, devoted and uxorious husband. Even
so, his marriage to Princess May was not initially easy: husband and wife scarcely knew one another and had spent
hardly any time together alone, they would never be good
or at ease in talking about their innermost feelings, and
their later declarations of the love that emerged between
them were usually conveyed by letter. Moreover, like many
royal brides before and since, Princess May did not find her
husband's tribe easy or accommodating, and it proved
impossible for her to establish warm or intimate relations
with any of them. Queen Victoria was affectionate and

welcoming, but also an intimidating and formidable matriarch, while the Prince of Wales was more interested in his
mistresses than in his only daughter-in-law, and Princess
Alix could scarcely conceal her jealousy of her son's new
wife. Her three daughters were also resentful of their
sister-in-law, envying May's superior talents and education,
mistaking her shyness for arrogance, and making unkind
remarks about her ugly hands and her morganatic blood.
Thus disparaged and undermined, Princess May became
ever more inhibited and formal in her public manner,
retreating behind an increasingly impenetrable facade of
stiffness and grandeur. (The American-born Conservative
MP Henry Channon would later claim that conversing
with her was like 'talking to St Paul's Cathedral'.[17]) Even to
those who were well disposed, she seemed to lack social
ease; while those who disliked her found ample cause to
dismiss her as dull. And for all her husband's loving loyalty,
he expected his May to be completely obedient, as, indeed,
she would be throughout their marriage.

One indication of such assumed wifely obsequiousness
was that the newly titled and newly wed Duke of York
had taken command of the decorating and furnishing of
York Cottage, which would be his family's home on the
Sandringham estate for the next thirty-three years: it never
occurred to him that Princess May, who knew much
more about such matters than he did, might be consulted
or involved. In scale and style, the house resembled a
good-sized suburban villa, the furniture came from Maples
and the pictures were reproductions from the Royal Acad-
emy; it was the same at York House in St James's Palace,

which the duke had also refurbished on his own initiative. Neither place was grand or stylish, reflecting not only his lifelong indifference to aesthetics, but also his dislike of entertaining and of London high society. Unlike his father, who was restless, cosmopolitan and liked plutocratic friends, the Duke of York preferred the settled, secluded life of a Norfolk country gentleman at Sandringham. The estate was the Prince of Wales's personal possession, originally bought as a retreat where he might be free from his mother's censorious eye; he subsequently rebuilt the big house, and created one of the finest sporting properties in the country. The Duke of York was merely a tenant, but this enabled him to indulge his lifelong passion for shooting. By common consent, he was one of the finest shots of his generation, and he delighted in slaughtering thousands of birds. Indeed, during the years between his marriage and accession, this was his principal activity, and although he made plain he was 'always ready to do what the Queen wishes or anything that may in any way benefit my country', he undertook few public engagements, at home or abroad.[18]

However limited and self-contained his life, both in London and at Sandringham, the Duke of York was now in direct line of succession to the British imperial throne, yet apart from his years in the navy and his visits to many parts of the empire, this was a position for which he had yet received no training. But what, exactly, should that training be? A Cambridge academic named J. R. Tanner, an expert on politics and government, was employed to give him guidance, and among the tasks he set the duke was that of reading Walter Bagehot's *The English Constitution* – perhaps surprisingly since it was scarcely complimentary to Queen Victoria or the Prince of Wales, and was confused and contradictory in its analysis of the sovereign's rights and pre-rogatives. The duke also had an obligation to ensure the royal line into the next generation, and this he soon and successfully discharged, as the Duchess of York gave birth to six children: Prince Edward (1894), Prince Albert (1895), Princess Mary (1897), Prince Henry (1900), Prince George (1902) and Prince John (1905). As had been true in his own case, the Duke of York found himself at odds with Queen Victoria over the naming of her great-grandsons; she had wanted the firstborn to be called Albert, but the duke stood his ground, insisting that his eldest son should be named after his own late brother. Following the birth of Prince Henry, the call of imperial duty intruded: not from South Africa, where the reverses and humiliations of the Boer War seem to have impinged little on life at York Cottage, but from the recently federated Australia, where the duke and duchess were invited to open the new Commonwealth Parliament on behalf of the sovereign. Then, in January 1901, as they were preparing to leave for the Antipodes, the Victorian age finally came to an end. 'Our beloved Queen and Grandmama,' the duke confided to his diary, 'one of the greatest women who ever lived, passed peacefully away.'[19]

2
Edwardian Heir

1901–1910

To the public he was not yet a familiar figure, but wherever he went he attracted affection, for he radiated friendliness and courtesy.

John Buchan, *The King's Grace*[1]

With the death of Queen Victoria and the accession of her eldest son as King Edward VII, the Duke of York became heir to what was still, despite recent anxieties and growing concerns, the greatest royal inheritance anywhere in the world. As the next in line, he now became Duke of Cornwall as well as of York, enjoying a substantial income from the duchy estates; he acquired a private secretary, Sir Arthur Bigge, who had previously held that post under Queen Victoria; he was given his own places near Windsor Castle and on the Balmoral estate; and he moved into Marlborough House in London, where he relented and allowed Princess May to superintend the redecoration; but he refused to take over Osborne or rent a large mansion in Norfolk, preferring to remain in York Cottage on the Sandringham estate. During King Edward's brief reign, relations between sovereign and son continued to be close and affectionate, in a manner unprecedented in the royal family since the Hanoverian succession. 'I have always tried,' Bertie had written to George shortly before he succeeded, 'to look upon you far more as a brother than a son, though I never had occasion to blame you for any want of filial duty'; and at his coronation, after the duke had paid homage, the king pulled him back, and kissed him twice in a gesture of touching emotion.[2] Whatever his shortcomings as a husband, and despite his outbursts of temper, Bertie had been determined as a father to treat his son and heir better than his parents had treated him, which may help explain why they had much in common: an obsession with punctuality, an addiction to smoking, a passion for uniforms and medals, and a devotion to the competitive killing of thousands of pheasants, partridge and other birds.

Yet for all their closeness and shared interests, father and son also differed from each other in many ways. Their views on sex, women and marriage were utterly unalike: the Duke of York never belonged to his father's 'Marlborough House set'; and he showed no interest in any wife but his own. King Edward continued his lifelong practices of eating and drinking to excess, and he loved high society, but his son remained slim and abstemious, and never liked entertaining, either in London or Norfolk. The two men also held decidedly different views on the politics and personalities of the day. In reaction to his mother's late-life infatuation with Disraelian Conservatism and Lord Salisbury's Unionism, the former Prince of Wales was more sympathetic to Liberalism, and he genuinely warmed to

Gladstone: not only on account of his politics, but also because he, like the prince, had often incurred Queen Victoria's wrath. By contrast, the Duke of York was an instinctive Tory, and would become notorious for his loud and indiscreet denunciations of Asquith, Lloyd George, Winston Churchill and the Liberal government that took office in late 1905. He also supported Lord Charles Beresford in the bitter disputes that raged over naval policy, while King Edward (who had bedded Beresford's wife) was on the side of the First Sea Lord, Admiral 'Jackie' Fisher. But despite their political differences, the king was determined to help his son prepare for the throne in a way that Victoria had never countenanced in his own case: he commanded that the Duke of York should receive Cabinet and Foreign Office papers and meet politicians of both parties. The result was that, although he had been woefully ill-educated, the Duke of York would come to the throne better informed and more experienced than his father had been – and, indeed, than his own two kingly sons would later be.

There was another area of interest where the two men differed: for while Edward VII was more attracted to Europe than to the empire, the priorities were exactly the reverse in his son's case. On the death of Queen Victoria, the journey of the Duke and Duchess of York to Australia had been postponed, and the new king, not wishing to be separated from his son and heir for many months, had no desire for it to be revived. But the government insisted that the visit was a vital and urgent reaffirmation of the essential links between the British monarchy and the British Empire, and so in March 1901 the duke and duchess set sail on the

Ophir, an Orient Line steamship specially chartered by the
Admiralty. For 231 days, the duke and his wife were separated from their home and their children, and they covered
(according to the duke's predictably precise calculations)
45,000 miles, laid 21 foundation stones, received 544
addresses, presented 4,329 medals, reviewed 62,000 troops
and shook hands with 25,000 people at official receptions.
Their travels took them to Gibraltar, Malta, Aden, Ceylon
and Singapore; then to Australia (their prime destination)
and New Zealand; then to South Africa and Canada, and
finally home in good time for King Edward's coronation.
On their return, the Duke of York spoke at an official dinner held in his honour at the Guildhall, where he urged that
'the Old Country must wake up if she intends to maintain
her old position of pre-eminence' vis-à-vis the empire. It
was a widely acclaimed speech, and soon after, the king created his son Prince of Wales, not only because it was an
ancient title traditionally borne by heirs to the British
throne, but also in recognition (as he rather infelicitously
put it) of 'the admirable manner in which you carried out
the arduous duties in the Colonies which I entrusted you
with'.[3]

Yet for all his devotion to the British Empire, the newly
created Prince of Wales was also obliged to participate in
the ceremonial rites of passage of his European relatives,
even though he never fully warmed to the continent or the
cousinhood. Already, in 1890, he had accompanied his
father on a state visit to Berlin, where the recently succeeded Kaiser Wilhelm invested him with the Order of the
Black Eagle; and four years later the same royal pair had

journeyed to Russia for the funeral of Tsar Alexander III and the marriage of the new tsar, Nicholas II, to Princess Alexandra of Hesse (who had earlier turned down Prince Eddy). Within a few weeks of his return from his great imperial journey, the Prince of Wales again visited Berlin, to congratulate the German emperor on his forty-third birthday: a difficult task, given the personal tensions between the kaiser and King Edward VII and also the growing naval rivalry between their respective countries. In 1904, the Prince and Princess of Wales paid a state visit to Emperor Francis Joseph in Vienna, who since the death of Queen Victoria had become the doyen of European royalty. Two years later, he represented the king at the wedding in Madrid of his cousin, Princess Ena of Battenberg, to King Alfonso XIII of Spain: to the prince's annoyance, Ena had embraced Catholicism in order to marry, and the ceremonial was marred by a (failed) assassination attempt. Soon after, the prince again deputized for his father at the coronation of Haakon VII as king of newly independent Norway. In this case, the family relationship was even closer, since Haakon was married to Prince George's youngest sister, Princess Maud.

By then, the more appealing claims of empire had once again reasserted themselves, for in the winter of 1905–6 the Prince and Princess of Wales undertook another long royal progress, to India and Burma. It was their first visit to the subcontinent, a five-month tour that took them to Bombay and Jaipur, Agra and Gwalior, Lucknow and Calcutta, Rangoon and Mandalay, Madras and Bangalore, Mysore and Hyderabad, and ended in Karachi. The royal couple were overwhelmed by 'this wonderful and fascinating country', but for all the spectacle and splendour of the Raj, and the even greater opulence surrounding the rulers of the princely states, their visit was not entirely straightforward.[4] Having lost his long-running battle with Lord Kitchener, the commander-in-chief in India, Lord Curzon had recently resigned as viceroy; the handover to his successor, Lord Minto, took place while the royal tour was in progress, and there were some tense moments and tactless encounters. Like his grandmother, Queen Victoria, the Prince of Wales disliked the racial prejudice displayed by the members of the Indian Civil Service, he thought that the ruling chiefs should be handled with greater sensitivity, sympathy and consideration, and he urged that 'the natives' should be 'given a greater share in government'. But he also believed that Indian men treated their women badly, and that Britain's imperial mission was in essence noble and well meaning, and he regarded the Congress Party as 'a power for evil' which 'misrepresents every action of the [British] government and holds us up to the ignorant masses as monsters and tyrants'.[5] He was eager for British paternalism to be more tolerant and benevolent, but he mistrusted India's nationalist leaders, and had no sympathy with their aspirations to independence.

These extended imperial voyages, combined with shorter trips to Europe and the regular perusal of state papers and occasional meetings with the statesmen of his day, took up much of the Prince of Wales's public time during the ten years of his father's reign. But like his parents and also his paternal grandparents, Queen Victoria and Prince Albert, the Prince and Princess of Wales were also seriously involved in welfare work: indeed, the prince served as patron or president of more than four hundred voluntary societies, and with some of them his connection was much more than honorific. Here is one example. In 1897, his father had established what eventually became known as the King's Fund. Intended as a permanent philanthropic memorial to Queen Victoria's Diamond Jubilee, this was a charitable organization primarily concerned with raising money for London hospitals. On Bertie's accession to the throne in 1901, his son succeeded as president of the Fund, and in 1902, the year of his father's coronation, the Prince of Wales raised more than £600,000 for it, with major contributions from the rulers of Indian princely states and Canadian plutocrats such as Lord Strathcona and Mount Royal. By 1910, the Fund's total assets were nearly £2 million, and it was distributing about £150,000 a year to the voluntary hospitals of London, which was over 10 per cent of their combined income. At the same time, and here was a portent for his own reign, the Prince of Wales also succeeded in saving considerable sums from his income as Duke of Cornwall, which enabled him to create his own private fortune: charity was not only to be carried on to the benefit of the sovereign's disadvantaged subjects, but it also began at home.

In addition to sponsoring and supporting good causes, the Prince and Princess of Wales also undertook a limited number of domestic public engagements. Some were primarily political, following the precedent of their earlier visit to Ireland in 1897. Others were described by *The Times* as 'welfare missions', as in June 1909, when they journeyed to the Phoenix Tin Mines near the Cheesewring in Cornwall, where large crowds witnessed the prince descending into a mine shaft in oilskins and later consoling an injured miner.[6] But for most of his time during the 1900s, the prince continued to lead the life of a Norfolk country gentleman, 'unostentatious, comparatively retired, almost obscure', interrupted by necessary periods of residence in London, at Windsor and at Balmoral.[7] The appeal of the Sandringham estate remained the unrivalled opportunities it afforded for shooting tame game birds; but by this time, the Prince of Wales had taken up another pastime that would also be lifelong, and that was stamp collecting. He had begun to show an interest in philately during the 1890s, urged on by his uncle, the Duke of Edinburgh. In 1900, the duke sold his stamp collection to his elder brother, Bertie, and he handed it over to his son. On that foundation, the Prince of Wales would build up the most comprehensive collection in the world devoted to the stamps of Britain and the empire, and as King George V he would not hesitate to press colonial governors and high commissioners to keep a watchful eye on the appearance of new imperial issues. He preferred to strike a good bargain, but he could also afford to pay high prices when necessary; and by the end of his life, the royal collection amounted to 250,000 stamps bound in 325 large volumes.

The Prince of Wales's philatelic interests were not shared by Princess May; she despaired that he knew 'nothing about pictures or history' and she regretted that her husband lacked her own linguistic fluency.[8] But since he would one day be king, and since she saw her prime task as being to support him and thus the crown, she stoically accepted his

intellectual and cultural limitations, just as she meekly sub-
mitted to his non-negotiable requirements that she wear
only such clothes and colours as he decreed: hence the long
dresses, the toque hats and the parasols with which she was
invariably associated, the unfortunate effect of which was to
make her seem even more distant and aloof. In his own conventional way, the prince loved and increasingly depended
on Princess May, as evidenced by a letter he wrote after their
Antipodean tour, in which he thanked God 'every day that I
have such a wife as you, who is such a great help and support to me, and I believe loves me too'.[9] But he also took for
granted her total subservience to him, and his parents
continued to be distant and difficult in-laws. Princess May
was too serious and high-minded to be comfortable with
Bertie's gambling, philandering and generally philistine
attitude to life, while he was annoyed when she went to
the expense of redecorating Marlborough House prior to
moving in (even though he himself had spent extensively
refurbishing Buckingham Palace before taking up residence
there). And Queen Alexandra remained incorrigibly jealous
of her daughter-in-law, often slighting her in private and
undermining her in public, as well as openly criticizing her
in her letters to 'poor Georgie'.

However much he loved and depended on her, the Prince
of Wales failed to protect his wife from his relatives' hostility, and he could be rude to her and bad-tempered. He
displayed neither imaginative sympathy nor spontaneous
warmth in his relations with her, and as parents, both of
them were cold and distant in dealing with their children,
who were initially brought up by nannies and nursery maids.

For the young Prince George that had been no barrier to establishing a warm and loving relationship with *his* father; but in bringing up their own brood, the Prince and Princess of Wales were remote, unapproachable and inattentive. The prince regarded fatherhood as a task akin to that of a ship's captain: he was a watchful and exacting disciplinarian, he treated his brood as midshipmen who were perpetually on parade, his temper could be terrifying, and he struck out verbally and physically to express his displeasure. His letters to his children were laborious and pedestrian, and he indulged in the sort of sustained banter and embarrassing chaff which left a lasting and often upsetting impact. While he treated other people's boys and girls with a genial indulgence, the Prince of Wales's idea of parenting has rightly been described as 'quarterdeck discipline tempered by the equally alarming badinage of the gunroom'.[10] Even by the standards of her time and class, Princess May was also an uncommonly detached mother: she hated child-bearing and took no interest in babies, and she expected all her offspring to behave from the outset as tiny adults. Despite the cramped and confined living conditions in York Cottage, she failed to notice *for three years* that a nurse was physically ill-treating her eldest son, and was also ruining for life the digestion of her second-born.

In their own inhibited way, the Prince and Princess of Wales genuinely loved their children, but they were incapable of expressing their feelings for them in a demonstrative manner; their only daughter, Princess Mary, was her father's favourite, but he could be a bully and a brute to his boys. As a result, the young princes grew up in an atmosphere that was strained, regimented and, despite their mother's artistic interests, culturally philistine. There were hardly any books at York Cottage, and although Buckingham Palace and Windsor Castle housed one of the greatest art collections in the world, no royal pictures were borrowed to hang on its walls. Not surprisingly, the early education of Princes Edward and Albert was desultory and unsystematic; and it did not improve when, in the spring of 1902, the Prince of Wales engaged Henry Hansell to be the tutor to his two eldest boys. The son of a Norfolk country gentleman and an excellent shot (which would certainly have been recommendations), he had read history at Magdalen College, Oxford, and had been tutor to the Duke of Connaught's son, Prince Arthur. Hansell was also honest, conscientious and loyal to his princely charges. But, like Dalton before him, he was pedestrian and lacking in culture or imagination, and he taught his two royal charges very little: indeed, Prince Edward would later claim he was 'completely self-educated'. Yet once again, their mother did not notice what was happening to her children: 'we have taken no end of trouble with their education,' Princess May blithely observed in 1907, 'and they have very nice people round them, so one feels all is being done to help them'.[11]

Unlike Dalton, Hansell seems to have recognized his pedagogic limitations, and he seriously doubted the wisdom of teaching the royal charges by private tuition alone, while Princess May also believed that her sons should be better schooled than her husband had been. But she did not assert herself, and the Prince of Wales, although aware of his own educational inadequacies, took the view that what

1. Princess Alexandra with her two sons, Prince Eddy and Prince George

2. King Edward VII with the future King George V and King Edward VIII

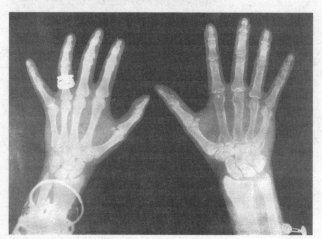

3. Queen Mary and King George V's X-rayed hands

4. Tsar Nicolas II
and King George V

5. *King George V at the Delhi Durbar, 1911* by
John L. Pemberton

6. King George V with the Prince of Wales, visiting a 'Gas School' during the First World War

7. 'A good riddance', *Punch* 1917

8. King George V entering a captured German dugout on a visit to the Western Front

9 and 10. King George V awarding the FA Cup and at the helm of *Britannia*

The thanksgiving Service ... attended by the King's Majesty ...

Their Majesties the King and Queen entering the Great West Door

O enter then His Gates with Praise

11. *Reception of King George V and Queen Mary at St Paul's Cathedral, London, Jubilee Day, 6 May 1935* (detail) by Frank Owen Salisbury

12. *The Lying-in-state of HM King George V in Westminster Hall, 23–26 January 1936* (detail) by Frank Owen Salisbury

had been good enough for him would also be good enough for his eldest boy. 'My brother and I,' he told Hansell, 'never went to a preparatory school. The Navy will teach David [as Prince Edward was always known in the family] all he wants to know.'[12] Accordingly, and having just scraped through the entrance examination, Prince Edward enrolled in May 1907 at the Naval College recently established at Osborne. For a boy of thirteen, it was an abrupt transition from the cloistered family circle in which he had grown up, but he soon got on good terms with his fellow cadets, and discovered how to charm and captivate strangers. He also showed a greater aptitude for French and German than his father, but the limitations of Hansell's tutelage were vividly evidenced by his weakness in mathematics and his total indifference to English literature. During his two years at Osborne, Prince Edward worked hard, but never rose beyond the middle of his cohort, and when he moved on to the recently constructed college at Dartmouth, which had replaced the old *Britannia*, his performance remained no better than average. He also found examinations difficult: 'I am not at all clever,' he wrote on the eve of his final tests, 'but I might pass' (which he did). 'We have done our best for him,' his mother breezily concluded, 'and we can only hope and pray we may have succeeded, and that he will ever uphold the honour and traditions of our house.'[13]

Such was the education deemed appropriate by the Prince of Wales for his eldest son, who would one day be king: but while the navy might have taught Prince Edward some of what he wanted to know, it certainly did not teach him much of what he needed to know. Nevertheless, the Prince of Wales was equally determined that his second son, Prince Albert, should follow the same path. But it was even less appropriate in his case, for he was not as robust as his more confident and increasingly dominant elder brother, being shy, sensitive and highly strung, and he was afflicted by chronic stomach troubles as well as a debilitating stammer. His siblings teased him about his speech impediment, and his father showed neither understanding nor sympathy, impatiently shouting at his tongue-tied son to 'Get it out'.[14] Although born left-handed, Prince Albert had been forced to write with his right hand; and for much of his boyhood his father insisted he wear painful splints on his legs, so he would not grow up knock-kneed. Such humiliating bodily interventions can hardly have boosted the boy's fragile ego, and may help explain both his stammer and his nervous displays of bad temper. But in January 1909, Prince Albert duly followed his elder brother to Osborne, where he found it much harder to adapt. Lacking the charm and confidence which Prince Edward had acquired, burdened by a frail physique and embarrassingly inarticulate, he was frequently bullied by his fellow cadets. His academic record was also dismal: in the final examinations he sat in December 1910, Prince Albert came sixty-eighth out of sixty-eight.

The navy was scarcely the best place to educate the two royal princes, but their father saw matters differently. For him, it was the senior and most significant service, and he would wholeheartedly have agreed with the Committee of Imperial Defence which declared in 1904 that 'the British Empire is pre-eminently a great Naval, Indian and Colonial power', and that the command of the seas was vital for its survival and cohesion.[15] Yet by the 1900s, neither the British Empire nor the Royal Navy seemed as secure as they had been. The Boer War might have been finally won, but there had been humiliating defeats along the way, nationalist sentiment in India was growing and in Ireland was reviving (to neither of which was the Prince of Wales sympathetic), while attempts to tighten imperial bonds by federation or tariff reform had foundered. The navy was no longer a greater force than all other fleets combined; the kaiser was determined to build more battleships and dreadnoughts than the British; 'invasion scares' were rife, and by the mid 1900s, it was reluctantly recognized in Whitehall that war with Germany might be unavoidable. To these accumulating international anxieties were added growing domestic concerns. Social surveys depicted at least one-quarter of the nation's population as being impoverished, undernourished and unfit for military service, and welfare provision lagged behind that in Germany. Support for the Labour Party was growing, trades union membership was increasing, and women were demanding the vote (to none of these developments was the Prince of Wales any more sympathetic). The franchise on which MPs were elected was one of the narrowest in Europe, and the Lords retained its veto powers over legislation sent up from the Commons, though not, customarily, in finance.

These were the vexed and pressing issues by which the Liberal government was confronted in the aftermath of its electoral triumph early in 1906, which took place when the Prince and Princess of Wales were away visiting India. King

Edward VII faced the prospect with relative equanimity, believing his new prime minister, Sir Henry Campbell-Bannerman, had formed a strong Cabinet, 'with considerable brain power' which he hoped would 'work together for the good of the country and indeed the Empire'.[16] The Prince of Wales was less convinced. He was amazed that the working-class John Burns was in the Cabinet, he was sure Winston Churchill would need a great deal of looking after, he thought Lloyd George a 'damned fellow' and he considered Asquith not 'quite a gentleman'. Even worse, 'a great number of Labour members' had been returned, which was 'a dangerous sign, but I hope they are not all socialists'.[17] Despite the prince's negative verdict, the new government, of which Asquith became prime minister in 1908, soon set about addressing the domestic, imperial and international problems it had inherited. The Morley–Minto reforms gave educated Indians a small part in the government of their country, and the creation of the Union of South Africa was an attempt to establish a fourth great British overseas dominion with Canada, Australia and New Zealand. The construction of dreadnoughts was stepped up in response to the German naval challenge, and the alliance with Russia in 1907, combined with the Entente Cordiale agreed with France three years before, effectively completed the encirclement of the Reich. Not surprisingly, the Prince of Wales was a reluctant visitor to Berlin in 1908, when he inspected a regiment of which he was colonel-in-chief; his subsequent brief trip to Canada, to inaugurate the Plains of Abraham as a national park, was more congenial and successful.

The new dreadnoughts cost a great deal of money, and so did such Liberal welfare reforms as the introduction of old-age pensions and the provision of labour exchanges. The Chancellor of the Exchequer, Lloyd George, needed to raise unprecedented sums, and in the spring of 1909 he proposed an increase in income tax and new land taxes, in what became known as the 'People's Budget'. By the standards of later times, these were far from punitive, but they were regarded as vindictive class measures by the Conservative, aristocratic landowners who formed the overwhelming majority in the House of Lords. Emboldened by their recent successful sabotage of several Liberal measures sent up from the Commons, but in ill-judged defiance of all constitutional precedent, the peers rejected Lloyd George's budget, on the dubious grounds that the proposals were unacceptably revolutionary. Asquith thereupon obtained a dissolution from the king, and in the general election held in January 1910 the budget provisions were subsumed in the greater controversy of the Commons against the Lords, and the people against the peers. The Liberal vote was much reduced, but with the support of the Irish Nationalists and Labour MPs, and much to the regret of the Prince of Wales, Asquith still commanded a clear majority. In April he introduced a Parliament Bill that would make it impossible for the Lords to reject a budget again and would also reduce their veto powers over other Commons measures to only two years. If the bill was not passed, Asquith insisted, the government would seek a second dissolution and fight another election on the same programme. Soon after, Lloyd George reintroduced his

1909 budget, which now cleared not only the Commons but also the Lords.

The parliamentary debates over the 'People's Budget' and the ensuing general election campaign were characterized by vituperative and belligerent rhetoric on both sides: the Conservatives denounced the Chancellor of the Exchequer as vindictive and dishonest; Lloyd George and Winston Churchill responded by ridiculing the Tory-dominated upper house for being full of rich idlers and parasitic wastrels. Despite his lifelong Liberal leanings, King Edward VII was appalled at the outbreak of such an unseemly class war, and at the extravagant denunciations of the titled, territorial aristocracy; and as an instinctive Conservative, the Prince of Wales naturally took the same view. There might also be worse to come, drawing the crown itself into controversy and contention: for what if the Lords rejected the Parliament Bill and Asquith requested the king to create sufficient Liberal peers – perhaps three hundred, thereby fundamentally altering the composition and the character of the upper house – to ensure it would pass? Early in 1910, the prime minister sought just such an undertaking from his sovereign, but this the king refused to give until after a *second* general election had been held. In taking that position, Edward VII believed he was supported by the Conservative leader, Arthur Balfour, who gave him the impression that if Asquith resigned because the monarch would not immediately agree to a mass ennoblement of Liberals, the Tories would be willing to try to form a government. Here was a potential constitutional crisis, centring on the issue of peerage creations, and thus on the crown as the fountain of honour, the like of which had not been seen since the struggles over the passing of the Great Reform Act nearly eighty years before.

Having opened the new parliament, in the aftermath of the general election, the king departed for Biarritz, but soon after he came back, in late April, his health suddenly deteriorated, and the Prince of Wales urged his mother to return from the Mediterranean cruise on which she had recently embarked. She arrived back in London just in time. On 6 May 1910, King Edward VII died, and his son and successor confided a heartbroken entry to his diary. 'I have,' King George V lamented, 'lost my best friend and the best of fathers. I never had a word with him in my life.' He faced his new responsibilities hoping God would 'give me strength and guidance in the heavy task that has fallen upon me', and encouraged by the thought that 'darling May' would be 'my comfort as she has always been'.[18] Meanwhile, and for the first time in the nation's history, the late sovereign would lie in state in Westminster Hall, so ordinary people might pay their respects before the service and burial at Windsor. In addition to George V and the German emperor, Edward VII's funeral was attended by the Kings of Belgium, Bulgaria, Denmark, Greece, Norway, Portugal and Spain. In retrospect, this gathering would be one of the last great public displays of the confident, cosmopolitan cousinhood of European royalty. Before the year was out, the Portuguese sovereign would be deposed; before the reign of George V was over, the crowns of Germany and Spain would be overthrown; and before the twentieth century was ended, those of Bulgaria and Greece would disappear. Domestically and internationally, the new monarch had many reasons to be anxious about the present and apprehensive about the future.

3
King and Emperor in Peace and War

1910–1918

The powers of a constitutional monarch must always be
indeterminate and delicate. But they are none the less real.

John Buchan, *The King's Grace*[1]

Despite the challenging circumstances under which he
became king, and the undeniable limitations of his education
and outlook, George V was better prepared than his father
or his grandmother had been when he ascended the British
imperial throne within a few weeks of his forty-fifth birthday. His accession was also an extraordinary piece of good
fortune in that it was he, rather than the hapless and helpless
Prince Eddy, who had lived to wear the crown, and it was
also providential that it was he, and not Eddy, who had
married Princess May – who, reverting to the second of her
baptismal names, would henceforward be known more
grandly and regally as Queen Mary. 'The quieter, easier time
we had,' she presciently lamented, was over. 'Everything,'
she thought, 'will be more difficult now', and so it turned out
to be, as the king immediately faced the most taxing domestic

political challenge of his reign.[2] Asquith's Liberal government, supported by Labour and the Irish Nationalist MPs, was steering its Parliament Bill, intended to curtail the powers of the Lords, through the Commons. It was sure to pass the lower house, but further confrontation with the upper house seemed unavoidable, and if the peers rejected the measure, the new monarch would be at the centre of a constitutional crisis. In dealing with this vexed issue, George V was in the unusual position of being guided by *two* co-equal private secretaries: Sir Arthur Bigge, who had worked for him when Prince of Wales, and Lord Knollys, who had previously been private secretary to the late King Edward VII. Their combined experience was extensive, but they would not always agree in the advice they tendered their sovereign, for Knollys was a well-known Liberal, whereas Bigge was a staunch Unionist.

Although Asquith was determined to pass his Parliament Bill, he was as eager as the new monarch to avoid a showdown between the Commons and the Lords, and so he suggested private talks with the opposition in the hope of averting it. Balfour agreed, and discussions were carried on from June to November 1910; but they were inconclusive, which meant the only way forward seemed to be to hold a second general election, and Asquith duly asked George V for another dissolution. If the king had refused the prime minister's request, Asquith would have resigned, and the king would have invited Balfour to try to form a Unionist government. But Knollys deliberately withheld from his master the details of the earlier exchange between Edward VII and Balfour: in part because by this time Balfour seemed to have changed his mind, and in part because

Knollys rightly believed the king must take the official advice of his ministers. Since there seemed to be no alternative, George V accordingly granted Asquith's request. But the Cabinet further insisted the king must *privately* agree that if the Liberals were again returned with a working Commons majority, he would be willing to sanction the creation of sufficient new peers to ensure the Parliament Bill would be passed by the upper house, even if the Unionist peers still opposed it. This request was partly motivated by political anxiety and necessity: the king's dislike of the Liberals was well known, and the Cabinet was anxious to obtain a definite undertaking from him. Yet Asquith also hoped that, if a second election again returned his colleagues to power, the Lords would agree to pass the Parliament Bill, in which case there would be no need for the mass creation of Liberal peers, and thus no reason for revealing that the king had been willing to sanction it.

At this point, George V received conflicting advice from his private secretaries: Knollys urged him to accede to the Cabinet's request for a confidential pledge, because it had been made to shield the king from public controversy; whereas Bigge advised him to reject it, on the grounds that it would be unconstitutional to give such 'contingent guarantees'.[3] But Asquith and the Cabinet stood firm, and the king reluctantly agreed to provide the secret understanding they sought, for, as he admitted, 'this was the only alternative to the cabinet resigning, which at this moment would be disastrous'.[4] At the ensuing general election held in December 1910, the Liberals were returned with a slightly increased working majority, and they accordingly reintroduced the

Parliament Bill early in the following year. By May 1911, it had again passed through all its stages in the Commons, but in July the Unionist peers carried a series of wrecking amendments, to which the government responded by asking the king to honour his promise to authorize the immediate creation of Liberal peers. Although prepared to redeem his pledge, George V pleaded for further delay, in the hope that the Unionist peers might yet be persuaded to let the measure pass, which would render unnecessary the flooding of the upper house with (as he saw it) too many inappropriately ennobled Liberals. To this end, the king's private undertaking was now made public, so the Unionist peers should be in no doubt as to the consequences of their continued intransigence. As a result, three hundred of them agreed to abstain, and despite the continued opposition of the die-hard Unionists, the Parliament Bill was eventually passed by a majority of seventeen. 'It is,' the king noted, 'a great relief to me, and I am spared any further humiliation by a creation of peers.'[5]

The protracted political crisis that was eventually resolved by the passing of the Parliament Act in August 1911 pre-occupied the king during the early months of his reign, and caused him serious insomnia (he was also afflicted with indigestion and toothache). But at the same time, the new sovereign and his consort were confronted with the task of establishing themselves on their thrones. One immediate task was to settle the financial arrangements of the new monarch. As king, George V retained the personal wealth he had accumulated from the surplus revenues he had previously derived from the Duchy of Cornwall, and he would henceforward enjoy the income provided by the Duchy of

Lancaster. He would also be given an annual grant of £147,000 from the government's Civil List, to defray the costs incurred as he performed his official duties as monarch, and other members of the royal family would receive between them an additional £146,000 each year from the same source. Since the reign of Queen Victoria, the monarch's grant from the Civil List had been subject to income tax, and Edward VII's advisers had failed in their repeated attempts to secure an exemption from the Treasury. But although Lloyd George did not like the new king (he once complained, after a summer ministerial visit north of the border, that the 'whole atmosphere' at Balmoral 'reeks of Toryism'[6]), he was eager, as Chancellor of the Exchequer, to humour him in such contentious times: and so he agreed to abolish the taxes levied on the Civil List, and also to secure the monarch's exemption from the new exactions proposed in the 'People's Budget', provided that in exchange George V would defray the cost of his state visits overseas, and also the expense of visits by foreign heads of state to Britain. This was a good deal for the sovereign, but it may also have reinforced his general reluctance to go 'abroad'.

There were also the new royal living arrangements to be settled. Queen Alexandra was uneager to leave Buckingham Palace; it was not until the end of 1910 that she departed for Marlborough House and the new king and queen were able to move in (enabling Queen Mary to deploy her skills at interior decoration once more). Balmoral immediately became King George's personal property, but King Edward VII had bequeathed Sandringham to his wife for her lifetime, which meant that King George, Queen Mary and their family were still confined to the cramped quarters of York Cottage. The royal style of entertaining was markedly different from that which it succeeded: the plutocrats and the smart set disappeared from the court, along with Edwardian opulence and ostentation. 'Nothing can be quieter or more domestic,' Lord Esher observed. 'We have reverted to the ways of Queen Victoria.'[7] But at Sandringham, the competitive carnage with shotguns continued. 'One sees pheasants everywhere in the park and gardens,' noted a visiting parson; 'the place is literally crawling with them.'[8] There was, however, a slight modification in the king's attitude towards his sons' education: Prince Edward's naval career was brought to an end, he was sent to France and Germany to improve his languages, and then to Magdalen College, Oxford, as an undergraduate; and Prince Henry and Prince George were sent away to a preparatory school at Broadstairs, on the south coast. (Yet there were limits to these new arrangements. Prince Albert went on from Osborne to Dartmouth and then into the Royal Navy; Prince John, the youngest royal son, suffered from epilepsy and, in accordance with the restrictive upper-class customs of the time, was brought up in seclusion at Sandringham; Princess Mary, like all royal women, was educated at home.)

But it was as public personages and ceremonial figureheads that the transformation was most marked in the lives of the new king and queen. At George V's accession, earlier rumours revived that he had married and fathered three children while a serving naval officer. In February 1911, E. F. Mylius accused the king of being a bigamist in a republican newspaper published in Paris and freely distributed to every British MP. There was no truth in the rumour, and the government successfully prosecuted Mylius for criminal libel. In the same month, the king opened Parliament in state for the first time, but although the occasion was relatively undemanding, he considered it 'the most terrible ordeal', and he always dreaded it thereafter.[9] Yet he protested too much, for in 1913 he became the first sovereign since the early years of Queen Victoria to wear the heavy Imperial State Crown at the state opening, and he would do so throughout his reign. The king and queen faced a much greater challenge in June 1911, namely their coronation in Westminster Abbey, for it was a lengthy and demanding ceremonial, it took place at the height of the controversy surrounding the Parliament Bill, and both King George and Queen Mary were visibly nervous. Yet the service was neither chaotic, as Queen Victoria's had been, nor postponed, as King Edward's had been: instead, it affirmed the sacred nature of the coronation rite and the historic continuity of the British monarchy, and also its recent transformation into an authentically imperial crown, as the standards of Canada, Australia, New Zealand, South Africa and the Indian Empire were borne in procession, and prominent roles were assigned to such imperial grandees as Lords Roberts, Kitchener and Curzon.

Although the coronation was the central event, the ceremonial inauguration of George V's reign was far from over. There was a naval review at Spithead, and the king and queen visited Ireland (the crowds were enthusiastic, but the royal pair would never go back to Dublin) and Scotland (where reports on the constitutional crisis gave him 'a lot of worry and anxiety'[10]). They also travelled to Wales, where the climax of their visit was the investiture of their eldest son, Edward, as Prince of Wales, in a newly invented pageant staged at Caernarvon Castle. Perhaps surprisingly, the moving force behind the occasion was Lloyd George: although he was a radical critic of the peerage, he was also the MP for Caernarvon Boroughs, and he regarded the investiture as a great local propaganda opportunity. The Prince of Wales always resented and regretted the 'preposterous rig' he was obliged to wear, but his father thought 'the dear boy did it all remarkably well, and looked so nice'.[11] Yet the most spectacular inauguration ceremony was still to come, for in November 1911 the king and queen returned to India, where a great durbar was held in Delhi, at which their imperial majesties appeared in person as emperor and empress, receiving homage from the proconsular rulers of British India and the indigenous rulers of the princely states. There had been no occasion like it before in the history of the British monarchy or the British Empire, and there would be no occasion like it again. The durbar was followed by an elaborate shooting expedition in Nepal, during the course of which the king-emperor killed twenty-one tigers, eight rhino and one bear.

No other British reign was ever begun with such an amalgam of European pageantry and Asiatic splendour, but the Britain to which George V returned seemed increasingly troubled and divided. During 1911 and 1912, trades union membership reached new levels, and there were national strikes by dockers, railwaymen and coal miners. As Lord

Knollys explained to Asquith, the king was 'very much disturbed by the present unrest among the working classes, and by the possibility, if not probability, of further strikes breaking out at any moment'; and he feared that continued confrontation might lead to 'political elements being introduced into the conflict which perhaps affect, not the existence, but the position of the Crown'.[12] The Archbishop of York, Cosmo Gordon Lang, who had become one of George V's few close friends, now urged that the king should come more 'into contact with the masses of the people', by visiting them in 'their own towns, villages and workshops'; and the monarchy's improved financial arrangements may have been a further incentive to increased public activity.[13] The tempo of royal visits was duly stepped up, as the king and queen travelled to south Wales and the Potteries, and in July 1912 they embarked on what was described as the 'Royal Tour of the North'. They stayed with Earl Fitzwilliam, at Wentworth Woodhouse, but their aim was to visit the local mining communities, one of which was Cadeby colliery, where eighty miners were killed in an underground explosion that tragically took place while they were there. At the same time that industrial unrest was growing, the suffragettes (many of whom were anti-monarchy) were also increasingly resorting to direct action: in June 1913, Emily Davison threw herself in front of the king's horse at the Epsom Derby, and died from her injuries.

However, the greatest threat to domestic stability came from Ireland, where the Nationalists demanded Home Rule in exchange for the support they had given the Liberals over the Parliament Act. Gladstone's second attempt to carry such a measure had foundered because it had been thrown out by the House of Lords. But the successful curtailing of the peers' powers of veto meant the way was now open, and in April 1912 the Liberals introduced a third Home Rule Bill, which the Lords predictably rejected in January 1913. A month later, Lord Knollys was retired, leaving the king with the strong Unionist, Lord Stamfordham (as Sir Arthur Bigge had become), as his only private secretary. Soon after, the Home Rule Bill was reintroduced in the Commons, and by the summer of 1913 it had again been approved by the lower house and rejected by the upper house. Under the terms of the Parliament Act, a bill passed by the Commons a third time could not be vetoed again by the Lords. But the growing hostility to Home Rule in Protestant-dominated Ulster encouraged Bonar Law, who had replaced Arthur Balfour as Unionist leader, and whose more intransigent views were sympathetically regarded by Stamfordham, to urge the king to veto legislation passed by such means; and as commander-in-chief, George V was also concerned about the dangers of using the British army to coerce Ulster into agreement, fearing there might be civil war. Asquith again retorted that the king must act on the advice of his ministers – or accept their resignations. But late in 1913, and urged on by George V, Asquith and Bonar Law began private discussions, and by the summer of 1914 they had reached some agreement about Home Rule being applied to most of Ireland, although with Ulster excluded for the time being.

King George V's involvement in the political and constitutional crises that unfolded between 1910 to 1914 was the most testing domestic challenge any twentieth-century British sovereign would face; and although he sometimes showed himself too friendly to the Unionists, he also demonstrated that the monarchy could still be an active and, indeed, necessary force in dealing with important and divisive issues. These continued controversies made it impossible for him to follow up his Indian durbar by visiting the four great overseas dominions as their reigning sovereign, but the tribal festivities and rites of passage of the European royal cousinhood were less distant and could not be so easily ignored. In May 1911, the king entertained the kaiser at the inauguration of the memorial to their grandmother, Queen Victoria, in front of Buckingham Palace: it was a family occasion, and only twelve months since Wilhelm had been in Britain for the funeral of King Edward VII. Two years later, King George and Queen Mary journeyed to Berlin to attend the wedding of the German emperor's only daughter, Princess Victoria Louise, to the Duke of Brunswick. Once again, it was a private visit and a family affair, but it was an extended royal gathering, for the Emperor and Empress of Russia were also invited. There had earlier been rumours that the princess might marry Edward, Prince of Wales; but although she had found him 'very nice' she also thought him 'terribly young, younger than he actually was'. More plausible was the closer liaison that developed between the Prince of Wales and Princess May of Schleswig-Holstein, whose brother-in-law was a younger son of the German emperor. In the end, nothing came of it, but in 1915 the prince remarked wistfully that 'I could very easily have done worse' – as, much later, he undoubtedly did.[14]

But these traditional, trans-national gatherings of European royalty could neither conceal nor eradicate the growing tensions between the countries over which they reigned: Britain and Russia were locked into the Triple Entente with France, and Germany and Austria-Hungary were bound together with Italy in the Triple Alliance. When the kaiser visited London in May 1911, he sought to obtain British support for German intervention in Morocco, which took the form of the provocative despatch of a gunboat to Agadir; indeed, he would later (but erroneously) claim that George V's courteous but uncritical reply to his request had constituted such consent. And although he was gratified to host the British king and the Russian tsar in Berlin, Wilhelm (again, erroneously) feared his two cousins were secretly plotting behind his back, wondering aloud why Britain had made 'alliances with a decadent nation like France and a semi-barbarous nation like Russia and opposing us' – anxieties which the king and queen's first formal state visit, to France in April 1914, can only have intensified.[15] Two months later, Archduke Franz Ferdinand, heir to the Habsburg throne, was assassinated in Sarajevo, and so was his wife. 'Terrible shock for the dear old Emperor,' George V noted in his diary.[16] In late July, the king was visited by Prince Henry of Prussia, the kaiser's younger brother, en route from Cowes back to Germany. The king said he hoped Britain might remain neutral, a remark the kaiser later misconstrued as a definite undertaking that Britain would stay out; but he also added that if Germany declared war on Russia, and France mobilized, then he feared Britain would be dragged in, too. Prince Henry's parting words were that if there was to be war, he hoped 'it will not affect our personal friendship'.[17] But there was, and it did.

Unlike his father, George V had never been much interested in diplomacy or international relations, he wielded far less influence than the kaiser mistakenly thought he did, and he happily left such matters to his long-serving foreign secretary, Sir Edward Grey. This meant he was largely an innocent and impotent bystander during the summer of 1914, while all the nations of the Entente and the Alliance (with the exception of Italy, which initially stayed out of the war, joining later on the side of the Entente) were inexorably drawn into the conflict. On Grey's advice, the king sent one telegram to Wilhelm, discouraging his naive hope that Britain would keep France neutral in the event of a German–Russian conflict; and he despatched another to 'my dear Nicky', urging restraint on the Russian emperor.[18] But neither the kaiser nor the tsar took any heed, and nor did their ministers or military advisers. By late July, the king concluded that it would be impossible to keep out of the war, if that meant letting Germany overwhelm France, and in deciding to uphold Belgian neutrality, the British government made plain it would stand by the French. By early August, the national mood was euphorically belligerent and crowds flocked to Buckingham Palace, where the king and queen appeared on the balcony to rousing cheers. On 4 August, George V held a Privy Council meeting to declare war on Germany. It was, he noted, 'a terrible catastrophe', but he was clear it was 'not our fault'. His final thought, as royal Europe headed towards disaster, was for his second son, serving as a midshipman on HMS *Collingwood*:

'Please God it may soon be over, and that He will protect dear Bertie's life.'[19]

The First World War confronted King George with many new challenges – as head of the nation and the empire, as a constitutional monarch, as commander-in-chief of the armed forces, and even as a semi-detached member of the cosmopolitan cousinhood of European royalty. Support for the war was widespread, and Irish Home Rule, which had seemed within sight by the summer of 1914, was postponed while battle was waged. From the outset, the king was intent on victory and in maintaining the peacetime values his subjects believed they were fighting to safeguard and uphold. For the duration of the conflict, Balmoral was closed, the shooting at Sandringham was curtailed, court rituals at Buckingham Palace were suspended, meals were plain and frugal, and in 1915 the king gave up alcohol. With Queen Mary, he sought to set an example of dutiful and patriotic encouragement, by wearing military uniform, and of unremitting diligence, by further expanding the royal programme of public engagements, which involved them in hundreds of visits to hospitals, shipyards and munitions factories up and down the country. The king also made more than four hundred trips to see British and imperial troops, both at home and on the Western Front, on one of which he was thrown from the horse he was riding and fractured his pelvis, which left him in lasting pain and discomfort. As a father, he shared the anxieties of all parents who saw their sons go off to war. The Prince of Wales served as a non-combatant officer on the Western Front, and Prince Albert was in action at the Battle of Jutland in May 1916.

Their younger brothers were also being trained for military careers: Prince George was sent to Osborne and Dartmouth, and Prince Henry enrolled at Sandhurst. (Prince John continued to live in seclusion at Sandringham, where he died in 1919 at the age of thirteen.)

Although commander-in-chief, King George was minimally involved in the military conduct of the war, but his own views were predictably conformist and unimaginative. As a former naval person, with decided opinions on the controversies and personalities of the 1900s, he was sceptical of the wartime recall of Admiral 'Jackie' Fisher as First Sea Lord, and relieved at his later abrupt departure; he was equally unhappy about Winston Churchill's conduct as First Lord of the Admiralty, he distrusted his audacious Dardanelles strategy, and he was delighted at his subsequent fall from power. Among the generals, the king disliked Sir John French, who initially commanded the British forces in France, for being too conventional and conservative even for him; yet he was unshakeable in his support of Sir Douglas Haig, French's successor and the scion of a Scottish gentry family with close courtly connections. In his initial hope that the war would soon be over, the king would be disappointed, as the conflict dragged on through 1915 and 1916, with unrelenting gloom for the Entente. There was stalemate on the Western Front, but also terrible loss of life, as at the Somme and Verdun. The hoped-for triumph over the German fleet did not materialize, as the Battle of Jutland was disappointingly inconclusive. Enemy U-boats threatened allied shipping, and there were fears that Britain might be starved into submission. On the Eastern Front, the kaiser's troops penetrated deep into Russian territory, and the tsar's army seemed increasingly incapable and demoralized. In Britain, conscription was reluctantly and controversially introduced, while in April 1916 the Easter Rising took place in Dublin – an abortive rebellion but also an ominous portent.

These military reverses and disappointments had significant political repercussions in which the monarchy was perforce involved. George V had not warmed to Asquith as Liberal peacetime premier; yet he became more sympathetic to him as he bore the greater burdens of wartime leadership, and he distanced himself from the intransigent Unionism which had been so marked a feature of the first years of his reign. But waging war was a task to which Asquith was temperamentally unsuited: he was increasingly criticized by the press and the Tory leadership, and in May 1915 he was compelled to reconstruct his government, giving Cabinet posts to prominent Conservatives. Encouraged by the king, he also created a Ministry of Munitions to which he appointed Lloyd George. But Conservative criticism soon revived, and Lloyd George came to share the view that Asquith lacked vigour and vision; by the end of 1916 plots to oust him were rife, and in early December the king accepted his resignation 'with great regret'.[20] In accordance with constitutional precedent, he then invited Bonar Law, as the leader of the next largest party, to form a government; but Law would only do so if the king granted a dissolution – which, in the middle of war, he was unwilling to do. After several days of confused political manoeuvring, George V called a conference of leading politicians at Buckingham Palace to resolve the deadlock, from which Lloyd George emerged as the only plausible prime minister. The king appointed him with reluctance, for he had never forgiven him for his earlier attacks on the House of Lords, and he showed little appreciation of his help with the royal finances; but he grudgingly came to recognize that he brought eloquence, energy and dynamism to the job that under Asquith had been seriously lacking.

The war effort with which the king identified was a conflict of nations and empires; yet it was also a gigantic family row, as the continental cousinhood was rent asunder, with the British and Russian royal houses on one side, and the Hohenzollerns and Habsburgs on the other. To be sure, King George V was insular in his outlook, and limited in his languages, and he was the first British monarch since 1830 not to speak English with a foreign accent. But in the increasingly strident and xenophobic wartime mood, he and his family could easily be depicted as being alien and German rather than British. An early indication was the campaign of vilification conducted against the king's first cousin by marriage, Prince Louis of Battenberg, who despite his name was wholly British and patriotic, but was compelled to resign as First Sea Lord in October 1914. George V deplored such attacks, and was reluctant to reciprocate by taking action against his foreign – now belligerent – relatives. Yet he eventually struck off eight enemy Knights of the Garter, including the German and Habsburg emperors, and he deprived both monarchs of their honorary ranks in the British armed services. He also changed the name of the British royal house from (the Germanic) Saxe-Coburg-Gotha to (the quintessentially English) Windsor, and members of the British royal family with German names and titles were obliged to change them to more English-sounding designations (Battenbergs became Mountbattens, and the Duke of Teck became the Marquis of Cambridge). 'The true royal tradition,' a Bavarian nobleman observed, 'died on that day in 1917 when, for a mere war, King George V changed his name.'[21] Nor did matters end there: for the king further decreed that members of the royal family need no longer wed European royalty, but could marry into 'British families', by which he meant the aristocracy (as, unusually, his sister Princess Mary had earlier done by marrying the Duke of Fife).

The result was a fundamental repositioning of the British monarchy, away from the traditional and transnational royal cousinhood and the personal friendships that had gone with it, towards the British nation and empire – a repositioning that the insular and monolingual King George V was well placed to engineer. A further indication of these changed priorities was that, in the aftermath of the first Russian Revolution of February 1917, the king went against the advice of his Cabinet, who suggested that Britain offer refuge to the deposed tsar and his family. George V preferred to put his country before his caste, on the grounds that it would be unwise to offer asylum to foreign relatives and failed autocracy, and thus he abandoned his cousin to the gruesome fate that would later await him at the hands of the Bolsheviks. It was a self-interested decision about which the king (and Queen Mary) would always feel guilty, and they would ever after be viscerally hostile to Communists and 'Reds'; but they had forsaken the tsar and his family, nevertheless. In the same year, and as another indication of the closer identity he sought to promote between the throne, the nation and his overseas dominions, the king created the Order of Companions of Honour and the Order of the British Empire. The CH was, essentially, a junior division of the Order of Merit, which King Edward VII had established in 1902; neither of them, significantly, carried any title. The Order of the British Empire was a yet more innovative addition to the honours system: there were to be both civil and military divisions; its five ranks extended from Knights and Dames to Officers and Members; it was open to all men and all women; and by 1919 it had been given out to more than 25,000 people. By turns, national and imperial, hierarchical yet also popular, the Order of the British Empire connected the king with all his peoples in new and novel ways.

It cannot be coincidence that these changes, in the identity and image of the British monarchy, and in the range and reach of the British honours system, mostly took place in 1917, the year when the character, meaning and trajectory of the First World War were all significantly transformed. In the East, the Russian royal house had been overthrown; the Bolshevik revolution portended a new hostility to European royalty; and the Communists accepted a punitive peace with Germany, which freed up the kaiser's army for one last assault on France. In the West, the Americans joined Britain and France at the eleventh hour as a co-belligerent. But President Woodrow Wilson did not take the United States reluctantly to war to defend monarchy, nations or empires: on the contrary, he wanted to make the world 'safe for democracy'. In Britain, where unprecedented numbers of men and women had been mobilized for military service abroad and war work at home, there was a growing recognition that the franchise must be extended, and the Fourth Reform Act of 1918 gave the vote to all men over twenty-one and all women over thirty. Whether he liked it or not (and he probably did not like it very much), George V was henceforward to be the king of that very 'democratic monarchy' that his grandmother had so disdained. But at least he kept his throne, which was more than could be said of the kaiser or the Habsburg emperor, both of whom were compelled to abdicate after their armies and their authority collapsed in the late summer and early autumn of 1918. Of the four great-power European monarchies that had gone to war in 1914, Britain was the only one remaining. 'Today,' the king recorded in his diary on 11 November 1918, Armistice Day, 'has indeed been a wonderful day, the greatest in the history of our country.'[22]

4
Revolution and Counter-Revolution
1918–1929

There was a clattering down of thrones in Europe, and the world was a little dazed with the sound and dust.

John Buchan, *The King's Grace*[1]

The king's relief and rejoicing at the victorious Armistice were widely shared throughout Britain and the empire: once again, the crowds cheered him and his family on the balcony of Buckingham Palace, and on five successive days he drove with Queen Mary through the streets of London. But George V also knew that victory had been hard fought for and dearly bought, and although most of his reign was yet to come, the baleful shadows cast by the First World War would not lift while he remained on the throne. More than 900,000 men from the nation and the empire had been killed during the conflict, which made the period during which he reigned uniquely deadly and destructive: under no previous English or British monarch had so many of the sovereign's subjects met violent ends. Hence the war memorials that would soon be constructed in towns and villages across the country and the empire; hence the unveiling of the Cenotaph in London and the burial of the Unknown Warrior in Westminster Abbey; hence the laying of wreaths of Flanders poppies and the two minutes' silence observed on Remembrance Day; and hence a new role for the king, in these solemn annual rituals, as the nation's and the empire's chief mourner. During the 1920s and the 1930s, Britain would be a bereaved and wounded country, and it would also be an impoverished and indebted country, owing millions of pounds to the United States – which, by 1918, had superseded the United Kingdom as the world's foremost industrial and financial power. The king did not like Americans, finding them vulgar, brash, materialistic and overly assertive; but he may also grudgingly have recognized that the leadership of the English-speaking world was inexorably passing from his side of the Atlantic to theirs.

Amid such trauma and tragedy, transformation and dislocation, the king's most ardent wish, like many of his subjects, was to return to the 'normalcy' which, at least in retrospect, had prevailed during the late Victorian era and the Edwardian belle époque before the lights had gone out in 1914. At Buckingham Palace and Windsor, court life was fully and rigidly resumed, governed by strict etiquette and protocol: the wearing of spectacles was still banned; ladies were presented wearing trains and feathers; and there were interminable conflicts over precedence and jurisdiction between the Lord Chamberlain, the Lord Steward and the Master of the Horse. 'The German War,' Lord Hankey complained, 'was a trifle compared with this.'[2] Balmoral was reopened in 1919, and at Sandringham Queen Alexandra continued to live on an Edwardian scale of extravagance, accompanied by her unmarried daughter, Princess Victoria, and frequently visited by her sister, the dowager Russian empress, Marie (who had survived the Revolution), and her daughter, Queen Maud of Denmark (who returned every summer to her house on the estate). Only on Queen Alexandra's death in 1925 did the king and his family vacate York Cottage and finally move into the big house. Throughout George V's reign, Sandringham always cost more to maintain than it generated in rents; but it remained his favourite residence, just as shooting remained his favourite recreation, and during the 1920s the bag of game birds would average 20,000 a year. Thus was the Edwardian and late-Victorian world reinstated; and when in 1927 the Great Western Railway introduced a new class of steam locomotives, honouring British monarchs, which for all their impressive power were very Victorian in appearance, it seemed appropriate the first was named *King George V*.

But such sought-after and contrived continuities in the royal homes and household could not disguise the scale of the changes that the war had brought about, which were vividly illustrated in the case of the king's far-flung realms. In 1914, Britain had declared war on behalf of the whole empire, and the four dominions and India had all responded to the mother country's call for help, especially in the case of Canada, Australia and New Zealand. From this perspective, the First World War had brought the empire together in ways no politician had previously succeeded in doing. Moreover, the victorious post-war settlements meant the British Empire reached its greatest territorial extent, as it was assigned mandates by the League of Nations over Iraq, Transjordan, Palestine and the former German East Africa, thereby creating an 'all-red route' from the Persian Gulf, via Cairo, to Cape Town. But in return for supporting the mother country, the dominion leaders had demanded a corresponding say in the policy-making and the formulation of strategy, and they got it. Under Lloyd George, the supreme direction of the empire's military effort was vested in a new Imperial War Cabinet, where General Smuts from South Africa played a particularly significant part; the four dominions were separate signatories of the peace treaties and joined the League of Nations; and Australia and South Africa were assigned their own mandates. There were also justifiable fears that this unprecedentedly large imperium was over-extended, and that Britain lacked the financial resources to sustain it in peace and the military power to defend it in war; while in India and Egypt (and also in Ireland and South Africa) there was growing nationalist agitation for independence. Sincerely but naively, King George believed there was a close personal bond uniting him with the millions of his subjects across the seas and around the globe. Yet it was not at all clear how such a vast and varied – and vulnerable – imperial conglomerate could be held together in the future.

The King did not wish anyone to 'interfere' with 'his' empire, but a new generation of nationalist leaders, such as Eamon de Valera and Mahatma Gandhi, would be only too eager to do just that. Of more immediate concern was the catastrophic impact of the First World War on royal Europe, where his three fellow emperors, all with titles older and with homeland territories larger than his, had been overthrown by violent revolutionary force: the Russian tsar had been killed, the German kaiser was exiled in Holland, and the Habsburgs' efforts to regain power in Hungary would be to no avail. Truly, there had been, as Asquith remarked, 'a slump in emperors', from which there would be no recovery.[3] Having been the natural order of things in Europe before war broke out, monarchy after 1918 was increasingly the exception, as it was confined to the western and southern peripheries of the continent, namely Britain, Scandinavia, the Low Countries, Spain, Italy and the Balkans. Of the crowns and thrones that *did* survive, several looked increasingly vulnerable. In Spain and Italy, the sovereigns entered into Faustian pacts with Fascist dictators: King Alfonso XIII with Primo de Rivera, and Victor Emmanuel II with Mussolini, neither of whom would further the long-term stability of their respective thrones; while in the Balkans, the monarchies of Albania, Greece and Yugoslavia looked distinctly insecure. To be sure, George V never forgave the kaiser for being 'the greatest criminal known', and he had abandoned the Russian emperor and his immediate family to their fate; but for the rest of his life, he would always regret that the stable, hierarchical royal world of his youth had been destroyed at the very heart of Europe.[4]

Yet as someone who had no flair for languages, and who disliked 'abroad', King George V was in fact much better suited to being a national and imperial sovereign than a fully participating member of a close-knit continental cousinhood of royalty. During the rest of his reign, he would pay only two more official visits overseas, and both, significantly, were to nations which had kept their kings: Belgium in 1922 and Italy the following year. But just as the empire and the continent were troubled in the aftermath of the First World War, the United Kingdom was no longer the stable, settled and secure place the king had known in his youth. The House of Lords had lost its veto powers under the Parliament Act, and after 1918 the House of Commons was elected on a mass adult franchise. The aristocracy and gentry no longer formed the natural, unchallenged ruling class: they had suffered disproportionate losses during the First World War, and after 1918 there was a 'revolution in landowning', as many great estates were put on the market.[5] More generally, the impact of war meant that class barriers had weakened, as officers and men had huddled in the trenches together, and as grief and bereavement became commonplace experiences regardless of social standing. Gender relations had also changed, with more women at work on the land and in factories, and with their enfranchisement in 1918. To this was soon added the chronic disruption caused by millions of soldiers returning home from the Front, who found it hard to find jobs in the economic downturn that followed the end of the war, as a result of which, unemployment had reached two million by the summer of 1921.

Nor did Lloyd George's coalition government, which won a massive majority in the 'khaki' election held late in 1918 to cash in on victory, allay the king's growing fear that things were falling apart and that the imperial centre might not hold. George V had never liked or trusted his wartime prime minister, and that feeling was heartily reciprocated. 'I owe him nothing,' Lloyd George once observed of his sovereign. 'He owes his throne to me.'[6] The king was impervious to his prime minister's legendary charm, and he also disapproved of his slapdash working methods and his loose sexual morals, while Lloyd George considered George V to be dim, narrow-minded, reactionary – and ungrateful. During the years of his peacetime coalition, from 1918 to 1922, relations between the two men were always tetchy, and there were several issues that particularly vexed the king. The first concerned the award of honours, all of which were bestowed in the name of the sovereign, but about which Lloyd George was at best indifferently cavalier, at worst deeply corrupt. He handed out peerages in unprecedented numbers, and often to people of unsuitable character; he failed to consult the king before promising titles to certain political friends or financial supporters; and some honours were given in exchange for money, either indirectly in return for a large political donation, or blatantly sold in the marketplace by touts such as Maundy Gregory. All this George V resented and deplored but could not prevent: his position as the fount of honour was ignored and compromised, public life was tainted and besmirched, and the aristocracy was further diminished and debased.

The second matter on which the sovereign and his prime minister did not wholly see eye to eye was Ireland. The postponement of Home Rule for the duration of the conflict, the (failed) Easter Rising of 1916 and the imposition of wartime conscription had greatly inflamed nationalist feeling, except in Protestant Ulster. At the general election of 1918, Eamon de Valera's Sinn Fein party won 73 of the

105 Irish seats at Westminster, declared Ireland an independent republic and embarked on a campaign of terrorism against British rule. Here, to the king's dismay, was an unprecedented threat: to public order, to the unity of the United Kingdom and to the integrity of the British Empire. Yet Lloyd George had no coherent policy to deal with this challenge. He initially responded by sending in the irregular, paramilitary forces known as the 'Black and Tans' to suppress the nationalist uprising, but in 1920 he changed tack, passing legislation that established separate Irish parliaments, with limited powers, in Belfast (for Ulster) and in Dublin (for the rest of the country). George V opened the new Ulster parliament in June 1921, and made a moving speech urging all Irishmen, both north and south of the new border, to 'forgive and forget'.[7] Six months later, the British government negotiated a treaty with de Valera, which established the Irish Free State in the south as a separate dominion within the British Empire. The king hoped that 'now, after seven centuries, there may be peace in Ireland'; but instead, partition was followed in the south by civil war and a sustained campaign to sever the remaining ties with Britain.[8] 'What fools we were,' George V later regretted, 'not to have accepted Gladstone's Home Rule Bill. The Empire now would not have had the Irish Free State giving us so much trouble and pulling us to pieces.'[9]

Yet for all their disagreements, the king and his prime minister were both concerned, in the immediate aftermath of the war, that the empire was, indeed, pulling itself to pieces, with growing demands for independence in the Middle East and India, and for increased autonomy for (some of) the dominions. On the outbreak of hostilities, the British government had declared a protectorate over Egypt, which it had ruled indirectly since the 1880s; but this provoked serious nationalist agitation, and in 1921 Britain relinquished its formal control. Although it retained strong political and military safeguards thereafter, this was the first significant imperial retreat since the American colonists had rebelled in 1776. It was equally difficult for London to assert its authority over the new League of Nations mandates in the Middle East, where many people resented having been unceremoniously reassigned from one imperial master (the Ottomans) to another (the British). Not surprisingly, the appeal of Arab nationalism was strong, and in 1920 there were serious uprisings in Iraq. In India, the Montagu–Chelmsford reforms of 1918 had marked a further stage along the road to what was now the stated aim of eventual dominion status; but they were insufficient for the Congress Party, which demanded full and immediate independence, and between 1920 and 1921 Mahatma Gandhi led an unprecedented campaign of civil disobedience against the Raj. In South Africa, General Smuts's hold on power was also distinctly uncertain after 1918, and the Afrikaners, who formed a majority of the white population, were increasingly demanding that Britain's fourth imperial dominion should declare itself an independent republic. Even in (undoubtedly loyal) Canada, Mackenzie King was determined that his country should never again be subservient to British interests and policies in the way it had been between 1914 and 1918.

The fear that everything seemed to be going to ruin, in Britain, in Europe and especially in many parts of the empire, combined with an almost paranoid concern about the future survival of the monarchy itself, meant that George V and his courtiers contemplated the immediate post-war world with anxiety and alarm. The American president, Woodrow Wilson (to whom the king took great dislike when he visited Buckingham Palace), had made democracy and republican-ism fashionable as never before; and Lenin (to whom he took an even greater dislike as the murderer of his Russian relatives) had endowed Bolshevism and revolution with a similar allure. In Britain, H. G. Wells wrote to *The Times*, urging 'the overthrow of ancient trappings of throne and sceptre'; strikers on 'Red Clydeside' and in south Wales proclaimed their support for Communist Russia; and there was the terrifying prospect of a Labour government, which would be committed to 'the common ownership of the means of production'.[10] This change in the political climate was accompanied by an equally disconcerting shift in cul-tural attitudes. In the era of Lytton Strachey and the 'Bright Young Things', the Victorian values of discipline and defer-ence, which had underpinned the monarchy, seemed to a younger generation to be both hypocritical and outmoded, and even the once-venerated queen-empress had become an object of flippant ridicule. Two influential courtiers gave voice to these immediate post-war anxieties. Lord Cromer feared that the 'unceasing labours and devotion of the king and queen' during the war had been to little avail, and that 'the position of the monarchy is not so stable now, in 1918, as it was at the beginning of the war'.[11] Lord Esher was equally concerned, urging that 'the monarchy and its cost will have to be justified in the future in the eyes of a war-worn and hungry proletariat, endowed with a huge preponderance of voting power'.[12]

King George V fully shared these concerns for the future of his throne and dynasty, and in September 1921 Lord Stamfordham conveyed to Lloyd George the sovereign's fear that growing unemployment would mean discontent spiralling out of control, and that agitators and Bolsheviks, backed by Russian money, were 'doing their utmost to bring about revolution'.[13] This was paranoia, but it helps explain the systematic attempts made after the war to re-establish the British and imperial monarchy on a more sure and popular footing, one aspect of which was the search for greater financial security. Despite the hardships of the First World War, the scaled-back nature of courtly life meant that the king had been able to save considerable sums, and in 1916 he paid back £100,000 to the Exchequer; but he had still accumulated a significant surplus from his (tax-free) grant from the Civil List. Nevertheless, in 1920, Sir Frederick Ponsonby, the Keeper of the Privy Purse, asked the government for a significant increase in this annual payment, holding out the alarming prospect that the king might otherwise be reduced to 'opening Parliament in a taxi-cab'.[14] This was exaggerated and, in the context of rising post-war unemployment, an impolitic proposal. The government refused Ponsonby's request, but instead responded by arranging a one-off transfer from the Duchy of Lancaster to the Privy Purse, and by initiating a study of expenditure in the royal household which eventually resulted in economies of £40,000 a year. It also resolved that the annual grant paid to Queen Alexandra should in future be 90 per cent tax free, and that similar payments to the king's younger children would be 80 per cent tax exempt, while the taxes paid by the Prince of Wales on his income from the Duchy of Cornwall would be substantially reduced.

These were significant financial gains, and at the same time the king and his advisers sought to align the British monarchy more closely with the British people, by actively promoting it as a living power for good. As a devout man, who regularly attended church on Sundays, and as a husband and patriarch whose temperamental shortcomings were unknown to the mass of the population, King George seemed an exemplary monarch, providing spiritual and moral leadership – the father of his family and of his people. Public life was still deeply imbued with Christian ethics and connotations, and it seemed entirely appropriate that two of the king's oldest friends were Canon Dalton and Archbishop Cosmo Gordon Lang (who was translated from York to Canterbury in 1928). One further indication of his faith (and charity) was that the king revived the annual practice of distributing Maundy money, combining religious observance with concern for the poor and the aged. During the inter-war years, George V also became a resonant and emollient public speaker second only to Stanley Baldwin: constantly commending the virtues of duty and service, community and tolerance, urging the rich and advantaged to show consideration and charity to those less fortunate, and expressing heartfelt sympathy for the unemployed and those who had returned maimed and disabled from the war. No monarch before him had spoken so much to so many of his subjects, and in so doing, the king drew upon some of the best writers of his time: Stamfordham was no mean wordsmith, and on occasion General Smuts, Rudyard Kipling, Archbishop Lang, G. M. Trevelyan and John Buchan were all asked to provide material and suggestions. In 1935, an anthology was published of the king's speeches since his accession: it was the first of its kind.

But it was not only in his quasi-priestly role that King George V brought the monarchy nearer to the lives of his subjects: for in many other ways, he had more in common with most of his peoples than did the public-school and Oxbridge-educated politicians and civil servants who governed them in his name. The king was both hostile to, and ignorant of, the major cultural developments of his age, among them experimental novels, atonal music and modern art, about which he was famously disparaging. In the National Gallery, he shook his stick at a Cézanne, and he later confided to the director, 'I tell you what, Turner was *mad*. My grandmother always said so.' His own tastes were far less highbrow, since he preferred 'a book with a plot, a tune he could hum, and a picture that told a story'.[15] Unlike his father, he read a book a week, including political biography and the novels of John Buchan and C. S. Forester; and he liked the gramophone and the cinema, provided the music and the movies were wholesome and decent. He was also deeply sceptical of intellectuals, and almost wholly ignorant of science. In addition to his obsession with shooting, the king nurtured the royal stud at Sandringham (though he owned fewer winners than his father), and raced his yacht *Britannia* every year at Cowes (much more successfully). During the inter-war years, he also established the tradition of the regular royal presence as a sporting spectator at popular events: not just race meetings at Epsom, Goodwood and Ascot, but also at the football cup final at Wembley, test match cricket at Lords, rugby at Twickenham and lawn tennis at Wimbledon. As a result, the royal calendar and the sporting calendar were increasingly aligned, and through his recreations no less than his religion, the king got far closer to his people than his father or grandmother had ever done.

In the uncertain aftermath of the war, George V's assistant private secretary, Clive Wigram, urged that more publicity should be given to the royal family's provincial visits and imperial tours, and although the king detested newspapers, a full-time press secretary was appointed at Buckingham Palace in 1918. Royal reporting was both extensive and deferential, and the same tone and treatment were soon being purveyed by the newsreels. Throughout the 1920s, King George and Queen Mary continued their visits to the slums and suburbs of greater London. They also went to towns and cities throughout Britain, touring schools and hospitals, coal mines and factories. The Prince of Wales, although no social crusader, began to make goodwill visits to such left-wing strongholds as south Wales and Clydeside: 'I do feel,' he observed after one such journey, 'I've been able to do just a little good propaganda up there, and given Communism a knock.'[16] But it was the king's second son, the Duke of York (as Prince Albert had been created in 1920 after his demobilization from the navy), who most closely identified the post-war monarchy with post-war social problems. After a brief period of study at Cambridge University, he became president of the Industrial Welfare Society, which sought to humanize industry by improving the physical conditions of the workplace and by bringing employees into closer contact with their employers. He began an annual camp at Southwold in Suffolk, which brought together boys from public schools and others from the factories and slums, with the aim of promoting fellowship and understanding between those of different backgrounds. And he was also patron of the National Playing Fields Association, which aimed to improve the recreational facilities for working-class children in the inner cities.

Some of these endeavours were more symbolic than real: the Duke of York's camp was unlikely to heal the social divisions by which inter-war Britain was split. But during the 1920s, King George, Queen Mary and their children carried out more than three thousand public engagements, and their cumulative impact must have been considerable. Royal ceremonial occasions, which were both symbolic *and* real, also increased in number. In 1925, Queen Alexandra was given a modified version of her husband's funeral: she lay in state in Westminster Abbey (rather than Westminster Hall), and this was followed by a procession through the streets of London and interment at Windsor. But the most significant ceremonial inventiveness centred on royal weddings, which had previously been held in the privacy of Windsor or the Chapel Royal, but which were now transferred to the streets of London, with full processions before

and after, and to the Abbey, where the service was conducted. The first such matrimonial spectacle took place in
1922, when Princess Mary married Viscount Lascelles, and
it was a great public success. 'It is,' the Duke of York
explained, revealingly, 'no longer Mary's wedding, but (this
from the papers) it is the "Abbey wedding", or the "Royal
wedding", or the "National Wedding", or even the "People's
wedding".'[17] A year later, it was the Duke of York's turn,
when he married Lady Elizabeth Bowes-Lyon: the first time
a prince of the royal house had been wed in the Abbey for
five hundred years. In conformity with the king's wartime
decision, both Lady Elizabeth and Lord Lascelles were
members of British aristocratic families: as the monarchy
was becoming less royal, it was also becoming more cere-
monially grand.

These immediate post-war years also witnessed the most
systematic attempt yet made to reaffirm and strengthen the
personal connection between the British crown and the
overseas realms – a link of sentiment between sovereign
and subjects on which George V was not alone in believing
the future unity and survival of the empire ultimately
depended. It bears repeating that, after his Indian durbar,
the king had hoped to visit each of his four dominions; but
the domestic political crises to which he had returned, followed by the demands and disruption of the First World
War, meant he was never able to carry out this programme.
Instead, and once the conflict was over, Lloyd George urged
that the Prince of Wales should undertake an extensive programme of overseas tours: partly to give him something to
do, partly as a gesture of thanks for the contribution made

by the dominions and India during the war, and partly as an antidote to the disruptive forces that he feared were increasingly tearing the empire asunder. As Lord Stamfordham told the prince, 'the Throne is the pivot upon which the Empire will more than ever hinge. Its strength and stability will depend entirely on its occupant.'[18] Hence, between 1919 and 1925, his extended tours to Canada (and the United States), Australia and New Zealand, India (and Japan), South Africa (and South America). They were gruelling, exhausting and lonely, the public pressure was unrelenting, and the prince's private behaviour gave much cause for criticism and concern. Yet they were spectacularly successful in linking the monarchy and empire more closely than ever before. In public, the prince was charming and tactful, eloquent and charismatic – a film star as much as a royal personage; throughout the empire, thousands of people turned out to see him, and he received unprecedented newsreel coverage.

By the time the Prince of Wales had finished his demanding sequence of imperial tours, the political scene in Britain had changed dramatically. In October 1922, backbench Conservative MPs withdrew their support from the post-war coalition, and Lloyd George resigned as prime minister, ushering in a period of political flux which brought serious challenges for the sovereign and his advisers. The leader of the Conservatives was Austen Chamberlain, but since he remained loyal to Lloyd George, the king instead invited Bonar Law to form a government, which, after some prevarication, he did. However, ill-health forced his resignation in May 1923, and Law offered no advice on his successor, which meant the monarch had to decide who should be the next prime minister. In the end, the king chose the emollient but not very experienced Stanley Baldwin over the much grander but very experienced Lord Curzon, on the grounds that in a democratic age, and with the Labour Party gaining ever-greater significance, a prime minister from the upper house would be an unacceptable anachronism. It was a wise decision, which events would soon abundantly vindicate. But in the short run, the choice of Baldwin did not seem to have been such a good idea: for in December 1923, and against the king's advice, Baldwin determined to fight a general election on the subject of tariff reform, when he lost his overall majority. To be sure, the Tories won the largest number of seats, but they were followed by Labour, which now became the second party in the state, while the once-mighty Liberals came a poor and marginalized third. The Liberals (again led by Asquith) refused to support Baldwin, whereupon George V sent for Ramsay MacDonald, the Labour leader, and invited him to form a government. 'Today,' the king noted in his diary on 22 January 1924, 'twenty-three years ago dear Grandmama died. I wonder what she would have thought of a Labour government.'[19]

More to the point, what did King George V think of a Labour government? An instinctive conservative, who distrusted radicals and socialists, he loathed Bolsheviks and Communists, he thought most change was definitely for the worse, and that seemed to be more than ever the case in the years since the war. Yet the king was also able to distinguish between his own personal views and his proper conduct as a constitutional monarch, and his welcoming and conciliatory approach to Labour (he urged that privy counsellor uniforms could be quite cheaply obtained from Moss Bros in Covent Garden) was matched by Ramsay MacDonald's disavowal of his party's more extreme policies. The successful accommodation of a Labour government into the culture and processes of the British constitution must be accounted a considerable achievement on the king's part. Then, in October 1924, the Liberals withdrew their support of MacDonald, and in the ensuing general election the Conservatives under Baldwin were returned with a substantial parliamentary majority. 'I like him, and have always found him quite straight,' the king observed of MacDonald after he had tendered his resignation as prime minister.[20] Until 1929, and notwithstanding the sardonic strictures of Lytton Strachey and the alternative lifestyles of the 'Bright Young Things', Britain would once again be ruled by conservative Victorians. That was certainly true of Baldwin and his colleagues, among them Winston Churchill, whose earlier radical hostility to the king had been superseded by a warm appreciation of the dutiful continuity he provided in a bewilderingly changing world. These views were also shared by such leading figures as Sir John Reith at the BBC, Geoffrey Dawson at *The Times*, and Archbishop Cosmo Gordon Lang at Lambeth Palace.

Like George V, Baldwin's government wanted to return to pre-war 'normalcy', and their determination was proclaimed by Winston Churchill's decision, as Chancellor of the Exchequer, to restore the pound to the Gold Standard and at its pre-war parity with the dollar. The General Strike of May 1926 challenged such comfortable assumptions, and the king was 'very low and depressed' at the prospect of what would be unprecedented industrial disruption and class conflict.[21] Although sympathetic to the economic plight of the strikers, he was also in favour of strong measures to curb subversion and disorder, and he was hugely relieved that the strike was brought to a peaceful conclusion: 'it shows,' he wrote in his diary, 'what a wonderful people we are'.[22] By this time, the post-war crises of imperial subversion and disorder seemed largely to have abated, and the king opened the British Empire Exhibition at Wembley on St George's Day 1924. Egypt and the Middle East had been (temporarily) tranquillized, and the Congress campaign of civil disobedience in India had been called off. The demands made by South Africa and the Irish Free State for a legal definition of dominion autonomy were also deftly finessed by Arthur Balfour at the imperial conference of 1926, when he balanced the central concession of the dominions' equal constitutional status with a recognition of their free and willing acceptance of continued empire membership. But George V was not pleased, deploring 'all the new developments in constitutional relations' between the dominions and the mother country.[23] Yet imperial sentiment and dominion deference still held, and in 1927 the Duke and Duchess of York set off on a lengthy voyage to open the new Australian parliament building in Canberra and to visit New Zealand.

The king rejoiced in his role as the father of his people, but he never mastered the more immediate task of being the father of his children, and the scoldings continued unrelentingly. In a return to the conventional royal pattern of the eighteenth and nineteenth centuries, his relations with his eldest son and heir were by this time especially strained. The king disapproved of the Prince of Wales's liking for fashionable clothes, cocktails and night clubs, deplored his liaison with the married Freda Dudley Ward, was baffled by his delight in all things American, and resented (perhaps envied?) his star quality and his popularity. In turn, the Prince of Wales regarded his father as stiff, old-fashioned, hectoring and heavy-handed, obsessed beyond all reason with etiquette and punctuality; his clothes, his cocktails, his fast living and his Americanisms were all expressions of filial rebellion and rejection; yet he also dreaded the prospect of kingship even as he would be personally relieved by his father's death. By contrast, the Duke of York, for all his stammering shyness, had made a brilliant match: the new duchess brought her husband comfort and support, and encouraged him to visit the speech therapist Lionel Logue to treat his stutter; although she found her father-in-law 'a bit gruff', the king melted before the charm and charisma of his first daughter-in-law; and on the birth of her first child, Princess Elizabeth, in 1926, he became an almost doting grandfather.[24] Meanwhile, Prince Henry, after passing out from Sandhurst and a brief spell at Cambridge, spent the 1920s as a cavalry officer and enthusiastic hunter of foxes, and his father created him Duke of Gloucester in 1928. His younger brother, Prince George, had passed out of Dartmouth in 1920, only one from the bottom of his class, and at the king's insistence, spent nine unhappy years in the navy.

Not surprisingly, all of George V's sons had reached adulthood nervous and highly strung, irritable and short-tempered, and although Queen Mary's relations with her children eased somewhat as they grew into adulthood, and she became more friendly to them than their father ever did, it was by then too late for any of them to get really close to her. Only with Prince George would she establish some rapport, as he would be unique among her sons in sharing her cultural interests. Meanwhile, the queen's life with her husband continued as before: she did as she was told, and put up with a great deal. Duty and service were ever her watchwords. She found life at Balmoral excruciatingly tedious, and would have much preferred visiting Scottish castles and museums. Her husband's passion for shooting bored her. 'It was so stiff,' she said of one party, 'I would have turned cartwheels for sixpence.' His delight in yachting baffled her. 'The *Britannia* has just passed us,' she wrote one August from Cowes, 'and I saw the king looking very wet and uncomfortable in oilskins – what a way to enjoy oneself.'[25] If she expressed interest at dinner in interior decoration, the king would shout down the table: 'There you go again, May: furniture, furniture, furniture.'[26] Yet in the public mind, the king and queen were very much a pair and a partnership, in ways that King Edward VII and Queen Alexandra had never been, while in private she provided him with the comfort and assurance he clearly needed. 'I can never sufficiently express my deep gratitude to you, darling May,' he would write to her on the twentieth anniversary of his accession, 'for the way you have helped and stood by me in these

difficult times.' Then he added, revealingly, 'this is not sentimental rubbish, but what I really feel'.[27]

By then, he had more than usual cause to be grateful, for
late in 1928 George V had fallen seriously ill, and during
the uncertain months that followed, the queen was a pillar
of strength. No doubt as a result of his heavy smoking, the
king's lungs became badly infected, as did his blood, his
heart was weakened and he lapsed into unconsciousness.
By mid-December, he seemed near to death, prayers were
said for him across Britain and around the empire, and the
Prince of Wales was summoned back from a safari in Africa.
'Imagine,' he remarked, both in triumph and trepidation, 'I
could be King of England tomorrow.'[28] Eventually, the poison was successfully drained off, and after surgery to
remove a rib, the king and queen went to Bognor in January
1929, so he could convalesce. But there was a relapse in
May, he was still a sick man when he attended a thanksgiving service held in Westminster Abbey in July, and a second
operation was performed soon after. By the year's end, after
twelve months' long and dreary illness, the king was finally
pronounced better; yet he never fully recovered. Meanwhile, the Conservatives, having campaigned on the
uninspiring slogan of 'Safety First', had been defeated at the
general election of June 1929, and in the new House of
Commons, Labour was the largest party, although once
again, it did not command an overall majority. Baldwin
resigned, and the convalescing king, clad in a dressing
gown, invited Ramsay MacDonald to form his second
Labour government. But before the year was out, the stock

market crash on Wall Street marked the beginning of a savage economic downturn that would last the remainder of the king's reign, and would have widespread, lasting and (in many places) catastrophic repercussions. From late 1929, King George V was living on borrowed time; as, indeed, was much of Europe, the British Empire and the world beyond.

5
Depression and Jubilation
1929–1936

The whole nation, the whole Empire, is royalist today, not only in constitutional doctrine, but in personal affection.

John Buchan, *The King's Grace*[1]

The Wall Street Crash was merely the prelude to the Great Depression: an economic earthquake so seismic and so protracted that its impact and consequences would be felt far beyond the time George V had left to live and reign. The Depression would also spell the end of the efforts made during the 1920s by Western leaders, with which the king had been much in sympathy, to try to put the clock back and restore the world to what in retrospect had seemed the golden age of ordered and stable prosperity existing before 1914. That had proved an impossible task, for the First World War had seriously weakened the material and military props supporting British economic strength, world-power might and imperial dominion, and the Great Depression would undermine them still further. Moreover, it was not only for Britain and its empire that the consequences of the global downturn were economically so damaging and politically so portentous – and, in many cases, so pernicious. In some nations where monarchy had survived after 1918, the prospects now seemed increasingly bleak. In Spain, George V's cousin, Alfonso XIII, was forced into exile. In the Balkans, the Kings of Romania and Bulgaria took up with Fascist dictators, the King of Yugoslavia was assassinated and the King of Greece deposed. In the Far East, the Japanese military invaded Manchuria in the name of the recently acceded Emperor Hirohito. Elsewhere, totalitarian regimes were entrenching and advancing, as Stalin consolidated his grip on Communist Russia, as Mussolini dreamed of creating an Italian overseas empire, and as Hitler seized power in Germany.

The early 1930s were thus not a good time for monarchy or democracy, and they were more testing years for King George V, his people and his empire than any since the end of the First World War. The global slump in manufacturing and trade meant that, by the end of 1930, unemployment was higher than it had been in the immediate post-war recession, and it was still rising. The king had also been dismayed that MacDonald's government had restored full diplomatic relations with Communist Russia, and with more people out of work than ever, he and his family feared there would again be strikes, agitation, subversion and disorder, all financed and fomented by Moscow. After the failure of the Credit-Anstalt, the largest bank in Austria, it seemed as if the whole of Western Europe was facing economic meltdown. In July 1931, Sir Clive Wigram, who had succeeded Stamfordham as George V's private secretary, warned the

king that 'we are sitting on the top of a volcano', and that if
there was a further financial collapse, the minority Labour
government would 'hardly be able to deal with the situation,
and it is quite possible Your Majesty might be asked to
approve [the formation] of a National Government'.[2] It was
a prudent warning, a prescient prediction, and also the prelude to the most energetic use of the royal prerogative during
the king's entire reign. But as his own generation passed on,
George V had to face these harsh and challenging times
with fewer friendly and familiar faces: among those who
died in 1931 were Princess Mary, Duchess of Fife, his eldest
sister; Canon John Dalton, who had progressed from inad-
equate tutor to the Dean of St George's Chapel, Windsor; Sir
Charles Cust, the king's oldest friend whom he had known
since his far-off naval days; and Lord Stamfordham.

As government spending rose rapidly, with more people
out of work and drawing unemployment benefit, and as
revenue from taxation diminished, Britain's public finances
looked increasingly precarious. From early 1931, MacDonald's Cabinet tried to devise a package of spending cuts and
tax increases that would be both acceptable to the public
and also to those bankers in New York to whom the government might need to turn for emergency borrowing.
However, many Labour ministers refused to countenance
significant cuts in unemployment benefit, and on 23 August
1931 MacDonald informed George V that he might have to
resign. But he also advised the king in the meantime to consult with Baldwin and Lloyd George, the Conservative and
Liberal leaders, while the king urged MacDonald that he

was 'the only person who could carry the country through'.[3] Thereafter, George V consulted Baldwin and Sir Herbert Samuel (standing in for Lloyd George, who was convalescing from an operation), and both expressed their willingness to join a national government comprising all three major parties and headed by MacDonald. The next day, the prime minister again went to Buckingham Palace, informing the king that the Cabinet had resigned and that he must quit too; but he advised his sovereign to summon Baldwin and Samuel to a conference, which he would also attend. On 24 August, MacDonald, Baldwin and Samuel met at the palace; and the king again asked the prime minister to remain at his post. Baldwin and Samuel agreed to serve under MacDonald, who resigned as Labour prime minister and whom George V immediately reappointed to lead a 'temporary' national government.

The three leaders hammered out a plan to cut public spending, which included a 10 per cent reduction in unemployment benefits. Many Labour ministers and most Labour MPs refused to support the proposed cuts or to serve with the Liberals and Conservatives in a national government, and they also disowned Ramsay MacDonald as a class traitor and a royal stooge. This was unfair. It was certainly the case that the king had actively and repeatedly urged the creation of a national government, encouraged by MacDonald's advice that he consult the other party leaders, and further reassured by their stated willingness to serve under the Labour leader. Had George V accepted MacDonald's resignation, he would have had to send for Baldwin and ask him to try to form a coalition government, but amid such uncertainty and confusion, the country's gold and currency reserves would have drained away as overseas investors lost confidence. So there was a strong case for the king insisting that MacDonald stay in post, and try to put together a national government to deal with a national emergency. Although he had underestimated the extent of Labour opposition to participating in such a coalition, George V had acted rapidly, decisively, patriotically and within the bounds of what was constitutionally acceptable. The new government, headed by MacDonald, and with Baldwin effectively serving as deputy prime minister, consisted of four Labour members, four Conservatives and two Liberals. As had been agreed, taxes were increased and state spending reduced, including unemployment benefit. But to the king's abiding shame, the naval ratings in the Atlantic fleet, whose pay had been cut, organized a strike, known as the 'Invergordon Mutiny'; there was a further run on the pound as a result, and Britain was forced off the Gold Standard to which it had only returned in 1925.

With so many of his subjects suffering from cuts in state salaries and unemployment benefit, MacDonald suggested that the king should once again set an example of sacrifice as (up to a point) he had done during the First World War. Accordingly, George V took a 10 per cent cut, of £50,000 a year, in his Civil List allocation for as long as the emergency lasted, and the Prince of Wales was volunteered (which he agreed to reluctantly) to give up £10,000 a year from the revenues of the Duchy of Cornwall. But as in the settlements of 1910 and after the war, there was also a rebalancing of the royal finances, the king being declared exempt from the £20,000 a year he had previously paid to the Treasury as tax on the income he derived from the Duchy of Lancaster; and in 1935, the cuts to his Civil List income were also restored. Throughout these years, the National Government, which had originally been formed as a temporary expedient, continued in power. Late in 1931, MacDonald had decided to go to the country, to seek a 'doctor's mandate' to take all necessary steps to deal with the continuing crisis. George V granted MacDonald a dissolution in October 1931, and was delighted when the National Government was returned with 558 seats, while an emasculated Labour opposition could muster only 56. The king thought it a 'marvellous' result, which showed 'that this old country is absolutely sound'; and he celebrated by taking his family to see Noël Coward's patriotic pageant, *Cavalcade*.[4] In a spontaneous outburst of loyalty, the entire audience rose at the end of the performance and sang the National Anthem. But the Great Depression continued to take its toll, as Britain's departure from the Gold Standard was soon followed by its abandonment of free trade, as tariffs were placed on all imported goods except those from the empire, and a preferential scheme for the dominions was worked out at the imperial economic conference held in Ottawa in 1932.

Although the pillars of the British Victorian world were falling about him, the king liked the non-partisan style of the National Government and the stability it brought to domestic politics for the remainder of his reign. Ramsay MacDonald was his favourite prime minister, and also the longest-serving; Stanley Baldwin shared his middle-of-the-road Anglicanism, his liking for country life and his belief in conciliation and consensus; while Lloyd George had been successfully prevented from making a political comeback. George V was also sympathetic to the government's foreign policy, especially its handling of relations with Mussolini's Italy and Hitler's Germany. He disliked both dictators, regarding the Duce as a 'mad dog' who was 'anything but a friend to England', and deploring the Nazi leaders as 'horrid fellows' for their anti-Semitism and repeated recourse to violence.[5] But even though the king was head of the armed forces, his hostility to war was also strong: he was against modern weapons such as aeroplanes, submarines and poison gas, and during the 1920s he supported the reduction – or total abolition – of all the Royal Navy's capital ships. 'I will not,' he exploded, as international tensions increased in 1935, 'have another war. I will not. The last one was none of my doing, and if there is another one ... I will go to Trafalgar Square and wave a red flag myself sooner than allow this country to be brought in.'[6] The king's ambivalence, between profound suspicion of the Fascist dictators and a pronounced wish to avoid a second world war, placed him foursquare with his government and most of his subjects. 'I am an old man,' he told his penultimate foreign secretary and fellow Norfolk landowner, Sir Samuel Hoare. 'I have been through one world war. How can I go through another? If I am to go on, you must keep us out of one.'[7]

George V was terrified at the prospect of another European conflagration, and as he once explained to MacDonald, he was also anxious about the continued unity of the empire. He had cause for concern. The Statute of Westminster, passed in 1931, embodied the formula for the dominions' legislative autonomy which Arthur Balfour had devised five years earlier, for it declared them to be 'in no way subordinate one to another in any aspect of their domestic or external affairs'.[8] Thereafter, Britain and the (essentially independent) dominions were only united by their common allegiance to the crown. The king did not like the new statute: on his behalf, Wigram called it 'a pedantic document drawn up by lawyers to satisfy the *amour propre* mainly of South Africa and the Irish Free State'.[9] It was a shrewd remark. In Ireland, de Valera abolished the oath of allegiance and the appeal to the Privy Council, and established a distinction between Irish and British nationality. In South Africa, General Hertzog had defeated General Smuts in 1924, and would be prime minister until 1939. Much more sceptical than his predecessor of the continuing British connection, he passed legislation in 1934 which declared his country to be a 'Sovereign and Independent State'. Even in Australia, the return of a Labour government resulted in the appointment, in 1930, and to the king's dismay, of a home-grown governor-general, Sir Isaac Isaacs, instead of the customary British aristocrat. During the 1930s, there was talk of sending out the king's four sons as governors-general of the four great dominions, in the hope of consolidating the links of sentiment which still existed between Britons overseas and those in the mother country; but nothing came of it.

In accordance with the legal decentralization and operational devolution of the British Empire, the king's title was modified so it could be separately used in all the dominions, including Ireland. The Statute of Westminster also meant that the succession to the imperial throne required the consent of each dominion parliament, and for the rest of his reign the king remained fearful that each of his overseas realms might pass different legislation on the royal title and the succession. To these anxieties about the dominions were added concerns about how India should achieve the identical status, as the viceroy had promised on behalf of the British government in October 1929. The king-emperor wanted the Indian princes to be supported and safeguarded, and the people to be happy and law-abiding. But Congress staged a second civil disobedience campaign in 1930–31 in protest at the lack of progress; three inconclusive Round Table Conferences were held in London between 1930 and 1932 to discuss constitutional reforms; and at one reception at Buckingham Palace at which he received the Congress Party delegates, the king vainly cautioned their 'rebel fakir' leader: 'Remember, Mr Gandhi, I won't have any attacks on my Empire.'[10] George V supported the National Government's efforts to frame a constitution that he hoped would gain the consent of both the Indian people and the Indian princes while also securing Britain's vital imperial interests. But the Government of India Act that was eventually passed in 1935 was unacceptable alike to many Indian nationalists, because it fell short of full independence, and to the rulers of the princely states, who thought it gave too much away. The Congress Party could not decide whether to accept or boycott the reforms; the ruling princes refused to join the proposed central federation; and the king-emperor was 'disgusted' with everyone concerned.[11]

Harold Nicolson may have been overstating it when he observed, in his official biography, that, between them, the

Statute of Westminster and the Government of India Act
signified the 'renunciation' of Britain's 'imperial mission',
but in the early 1930s King George had good reasons to be
as anxious about the empire as he was about Europe.[12] Yet
these difficult years also witnessed a triumphant innovation
that helped consolidate those links of sentiment which
undoubtedly still existed between the empire and the crown.
In 1924, and at the urging of its general manager, John
Reith, the speech delivered by the king to open the British
Empire Exhibition at Wembley had been broadcast by
the recently formed BBC. It attracted an audience of ten
million, and thereafter the BBC broadcast several of the
speeches that George V gave on ceremonial occasions; yet
until 1932, he repeatedly refused requests to deliver a more
personal Christmas message to his imperial subjects. But
following the death of Stamfordham, and his replacement
as private secretary by the more media-savvy Wigram, the
king was reluctantly persuaded, and after lunch on Christmas Day he broadcast live from Sandringham what he
described as 'a short message of 251 words to the whole
Empire'. 'I speak now,' he began, 'from my home and from
my heart to you all; to men and women so cut off by the
snows or the desert or the sea, that only voices out of the air
can reach them.'[13] The words had been written by Kipling,
but the delivery – 'strong, emphatic, vibrant, with under-
tones of sentiment, devoid of all condescension, artifice or
pose' – was inimitably his own.[14] For all his barking shyness, the king was a natural broadcaster, and what would
in the following year become the annual tradition of the

Christmas broadcast brought the crown into millions of homes across the empire.

The king's seasonal messages endowed the monarchy with a wholly new form of magic, as he spoke to his subjects in an intimate, immediate and reassuring human voice, and as they gathered, enthralled and expectant, around their wirelesses to hear him. But he was not getting any closer to his own children. 'Remember how your father,' the Duchess of York wrote to the duke at this time, 'by shouting at you and making you feel uncomfortable, lost all your real affection. None of his sons,' she went on, 'are his friends, because he is not understanding and helpful to them.'[15] The faults were not all on the king's side, however, least of all in the case of the Prince of Wales, who in 1934 reached the age of forty, but was still unmarried. To make matters worse, he had recently taken up with Wallis Simpson, who, having divorced and remarried, had *two* living husbands and was self-evidently neither royal nor even aristocratic. By the standards and conventions of the time, this made her completely unacceptable as a royal consort, let alone as queen, and the king was appalled and enraged by his son's latest irresponsible liaison. The prince was also vociferous in his oft-expressed admiration for Nazi Germany, and seemed to have acquired no appreciation of the constrained position of a constitutional monarch vis-à-vis his Cabinet. 'He has not a single friend who is a gentleman,' George V lamented. 'He does not see any decent society . . . I hardly ever see him, and don't know what he is doing.'[16] By contrast, the lives and conduct of the Duke and Duchess of

York and their two daughters (Princess Margaret Rose was born in 1930) seemed a model of private and public propriety, and in them now lay the king's best hope for the future of the House of Windsor. 'I pray to God,' he confided to a lady-in-waiting, 'that my eldest son will never marry and have children, and that nothing will come between Bertie and Lilibet and the throne.'[17]

Meanwhile, the king's two younger sons marked time, before both of them married – unexpectedly well. The Duke of Gloucester continued in his cavalry career, but was constantly frustrated that he could not join his regiment on active duty in Egypt or India, because of his royal lineage. Instead he was distracted with overseas visits: to Japan to present the Garter to Emperor Hirohito, to Abyssinia to attend the coronation of Emperor Haile Selassie, and to Australia to mark the hundredth anniversary of the first settlements in Victoria. Prince George, to his great relief, finally got out of the navy in 1929, worked desultorily in the Foreign Office and the Home Office, paid a visit to South Africa, and was created Duke of Kent in 1934. Uniquely among his brothers, he had inherited his mother's cultural interests; but he was also closest to the Prince of Wales in his liking for night clubs and fast living, and he took drugs and was voraciously bisexual. Apart from his royal status, neither duke had much to recommend him: Gloucester was shy, crotchety and disappointed; Kent was wayward and self-indulgent. Yet both made brilliant matches: Kent, in a throwback to pre-war practices, was accepted by Princess Marina, a member of the exiled Greek royal family; while Gloucester, like his elder brother, married into the Anglo-Scottish aristocracy, by wedding Lady Alice Montagu-Douglas-Scott, a daughter of the very broad-acred Duke of Buccleuch. In accordance with the precedents created in the early 1920s, the Duke of Kent and Princess Marina were married in Westminster Abbey, but the death of the Duke of Buccleuch meant the Duke of Gloucester's wedding to Lady Alice was transferred at the last minute from the Abbey to the private chapel at Buckingham Palace.

These two royal weddings took place in November 1934 (Kent) and November 1935 (Gloucester), and exactly halfway between each event the most spectacular display of royal pageantry was mounted since the beginning of the king's reign, as he celebrated twenty-five years on the throne. No British monarch had ever observed a Silver Jubilee before (Queen Victoria, who might have done so, had been in deep mourning for Albert in 1862), but the National Government encouraged George V to mark the anniversary, and it was celebrated across Britain and around the empire, with flags and bunting, parties and processions, speeches and services. On 6 May 1935, the king drove to St Paul's Cathedral with Queen Mary to give thanks. 'A never to be forgotten day,' he later recorded, in words reminiscent of those used by his grandmother at her Diamond Jubilee. 'The greatest number of people in the streets that I have ever seen in my life.'[18] That evening, the king broadcast to his peoples, thanking them 'for all the loyalty – and may I say so? – love' with which he and the queen had always been surrounded.[19] There were drives through the streets of London, a reception for the dominion prime ministers, a naval review at Spithead, and addresses presented by both Houses of Parliament in Westminster Hall. The king's reply to them surveyed the themes and restated the values that had characterized his reign: the development of the empire bound together by shared allegiance to the crown; the peaceful evolution of democracy and constitutional monarchy; the importance of the rule of law and of the impulse towards social improvement; the mortal peril of the First World War and the peacetime ordeal of depression, hardship and unemployment; and he ended by hoping 'that we may continue to pursue the course of freedom and progress in a spirit of peace, tolerance and understanding'.[20]

Like all such ceremonials, the meanings and messages of George V's Silver Jubilee were manifold and multifarious, for it was as much about the reign as about the king. It was an expression of collective gratitude for the constancy and dutifulness with which he had discharged his paternal responsibilities, as father of the nation and of the empire, which under his benevolent aegis formed 'one great family'. It was a recognition that his varied sporting interests, his visits to towns and villages, hospitals and factories, his simple Christian faith and his wireless broadcasts had brought the crown closer to the lives of his subjects than any monarch before him. It paid homage to a sovereign who had stayed faithful to his people in war, who had presided over the transition to full adult suffrage in peace, who had reconciled the Labour Party to the constitution, and who had successfully urged the creation of a national government to deal with a national emergency. It proclaimed that his dignity and decency contrasted so favourably to the dictatorial demagoguery of Hitler and Mussolini, just as the anachronistic splendour of royal pageantry seemed so much more traditional and dignified than the planes and searchlights of the Nuremberg rallies. It was staged as much to encourage the continuing devotion of the dominions and India as to celebrate national cohesion. And it acknowledged the stability, continuity and reassurance the monarch embodied in a rapidly changing world, as his reign had witnessed the disappearance of five emperors, eight kings and eighteen minor dynasties. As a tribute to the sovereign's popularity, and as a lasting legacy of his quarter century of dutiful service, the King George's Jubilee Trust was established 'to promote the welfare of the younger generation', which soon raised more than £1 million.[21]

Yet amid the pageants and the parties, the rejoicings and the encomiums, the gifts and the subscriptions, there were other conclusions that could be drawn from the jubilee that were distinctly less encouraging, for while King George V occupied the throne, Britain and its empire had passed their great-power zenith, which meant he was the first monarch of modern times to reign in what was essentially Kipling's 'recessional' mode. His grandmother's jubilees of 1887 and 1897 had been triumphant celebrations of national progress and imperial might. But there had also been early warnings of decay and decline, and by 1935 Britain was a relatively weaker nation than it had been in Queen Victoria's day. The empire was also less unified and more vulnerable, and this was made plain in two revealing episodes that took place during the Silver Jubilee celebrations. The first was the Irish Free State's refusal to participate in the king's reception for the dominion prime ministers: 'the gap,' Ramsay MacDonald wrote, 'lay like a shadow of smallness over a ceremony of bigness and graciousness', but it was also an indication that Ireland was seriously intent on getting out of the British Empire altogether.[22] The second was the naval review at Spithead, where the assemblage of 160 warships looked impressive enough at first glance; but this was no longer, as it had been in Queen Victoria's day, a navy greater than all others combined, and much of the fleet had been built before the First World War and was seriously out of date, while there were few recently constructed ships. The explanations for these naval shortcomings were clear and dismaying: the government had been unable to afford to build new warships in sufficient numbers, and Britain's traditional heavy industries were no longer as creative or as competitive as they had been before 1914.

Not surprisingly, the mood of the Silver Jubilee was more one of sombre gratitude than of jingoistic euphoria, both for George V and his people, and by the end of 1935 it had further darkened. For the king, this was partly personal. Although he hoped MacDonald 'might have seen me through', he resigned as prime minister soon after the jubilee and was succeeded by Stanley Baldwin.[23] The Prince of Wales remained besotted with Wallis Simpson; indeed, as the king predicted to Baldwin: 'after I am dead, the boy will ruin himself in twelve months'.[24] Then, in December 1935, his unmarried sister, Princess Victoria, died. She had become embittered and spiteful, yet they had talked on the telephone virtually every day, and of the five children of Bertie and Alix, only the king and his sister Queen Maud of

Norway now remained. But there were also growing public grounds for anxiety and concern. At the general election held in November, the National Government had again been returned with a reduced but still comfortable majority. By then, however, Italy had invaded Abyssinia, in flagrant defiance of the League of Nations; Haile Selassie, whose coronation had been attended by the Duke of Gloucester, was deposed; the Italian monarch was proclaimed as his successor; and in homage to, or defiance of, the British imperial throne, he would declare himself to be king and emperor. George V was appalled that yet another legitimate monarch had gone, and he could not sleep at night for worry. His chiefs of staff were even more concerned: for this display of Fascist aggression meant they now feared there might be a future war in which Britain would simultaneously have to fight Germany in Europe and on the high seas, Italy in the Mediterranean and north Africa, and Japan in the Far East. It was a terrifying prospect, since the empire would never command the resources to wage and win such a global war on three fronts.

The king turned seventy in his jubilee year; it would be his last birthday, and Sir Samuel Hoare opined that 'it was the anxieties of Abyssinia, coming as they did on the top of the Silver Jubilee celebrations' that 'killed' him.[25] In early 1935, there had been a recurrence of his previous bronchial trouble; by the autumn, he was visibly failing, and to those closest to him he seemed to be making ready to depart. He shot his last birds at Sandringham in November, cancelled the state opening of Parliament the following month, and delivered his final Christmas broadcast. On 17 January 1936, he wrote the last entry in the diary he had kept since 1880, and three days later members of the Privy Council gathered in the king's bedroom where, with great difficulty, he initialled a proclamation constituting a council of state. As his strength ebbed away, his personal physician, Lord Dawson, drafted a memorable farewell bulletin: 'The King's life is moving peacefully towards its close.'[26] Two accounts of his last words reflect the different sides of his private and public personalities. According to one version, another doctor in attendance tried to cheer up his patient by suggesting that, once he was better, he might again go to Bognor to convalesce, as he had done in 1929. To which the king allegedly replied, 'Bugger Bognor.'[27] Alternatively, and according to Stanley Baldwin, his final words were to ask 'How is the Empire?'[28] In the evening, the queen and her children gathered around the king's bedside, while the doctors eased his pain and may have timed his death to suit the morning newspapers. Just before midnight, on 20 January 1936, King George V died, and in homage to the new monarch, Queen Mary kissed the hand of King Edward VIII. 'Am broken hearted,' she confided to her diary, and later she would copy into it these words: 'the sunset of his death tinged the whole world's sky'.[29]

Tributes were paid to the late king across the nation, throughout the empire and beyond, and his death occasioned a widespread sense of personal loss among many of his subjects, who had never met him, and did not know him, but who somehow felt that they had and that they did. As Sir Austen Chamberlain wrote to his sister Hilda:

How well he has played his part, and what a place he has made for himself in the hearts of his people. I think that his broadcasts have made him more intimately known to his peoples overseas than any of his predecessors, and have strengthened the attachment of distant peoples to the throne.[30]

Although not born to succeed, King George had done so in both senses of the word: he had unexpectedly inherited the throne, and he had been an unexpectedly successful king (though a less successful parent). Deeply conservative and, according to his eldest son, waging a constant but futile battle against the twentieth century, he nevertheless accommodated to being a 'democratic monarch', he was advised and able to distinguish between his private opinions and his public obligations, and he dealt effectively with a unique succession of domestic political crises in which he was perforce involved. Less European and more parochial than his two predecessors, he was perfectly placed in the aftermath of the First World War to steer the monarchy away from the cosmopolitan royal cousinhood and towards the nation and empire – and even towards the Labour Party. Disparaged by highbrows and intellectuals for being unimaginative, philistine and uneducated, this gave him a rapport with the majority of his subjects that his Christmas broadcasts consolidated. And his understated Anglicanism, combined with his love of the countryside, would, once Edward VIII was gone, set the tone of the British monarchy for the rest of the twentieth century – and beyond.

Following the precedent established in the mourning for his father, King George V's body was brought back from Sandringham, and lay in state in Westminster Hall for four days. But as the procession made its way from King's Cross Station to New Palace Yard, the jewelled Maltese cross fell off the Imperial State Crown that rested on the top of his coffin. It seemed to many 'a most terrible omen' of what might soon be to come.[31] Nearly one million people filed by the late monarch's catafalque, and on the last night King Edward VIII and his three brothers, clad in full military uniform, briefly stood guard. After the gun-carriage procession through the streets of London, from Westminster Hall to Paddington Station, and the train journey to Windsor, the funeral took place at St George's Chapel, attended by the Kings of Denmark, Norway, Romania, Bulgaria and Belgium – their limited and marginal European realms a vivid reminder that Britain was the only great-power monarchy remaining on the continent. Within a few years, these thrones would face uncertain futures, and in little more than ten years, two of them would disappear. By contrast, George V had left his imperial crown strong and secure – except in one crucial respect of which he himself had been only too well aware. For about his successor, as Austen Chamberlain's letter went on to observe, people in the know harboured serious doubts:

> What will the Prince make of his task? I am hopeful, but he has been going downhill of late, and must pull himself together if he is to carry on the great tradition to which he is heir.[32]

Notes

PREFACE

1. J. Buchan, *The King's Grace, 1910–1935* (London: Hodder & Stoughton, 1935), p. 17.

1. VICTORIAN GRANDCHILD, 1865–1901

1. Buchan, *King's Grace*, p. 17. (The quotation on p. 2 is from *King's Grace*, p. 10.)
2. J. Ridley, *Bertie: A Life of Edward VII* (London: Chatto & Windus, 2012), p. 78.
3. Ibid., p. 66.
4. W. Bagehot, *The English Constitution*, ed. R. H. S. Crossman (London: Fontana, 1963), p. 82.
5. Ibid., p. 113.
6. G. E. Buckle (ed.), *The Letters of Queen Victoria*, 2nd series, 3 vols (London: John Murray, 1926–8), vol. 3, p. 166.
7. H. Nicolson, *King George V: His Life and Reign* (London: Constable, 1967), p. 28.
8. G. Battiscombe, *Queen Alexandra* (London: Cardinal Books, 1972), pp. 122–3.
9. J. Bailey (ed.), *The Diary of Lady Frederick Cavendish*, 2 vols (London: John Murray, 1927), vol. 2, p. 146.
10. K. Rose, *King George V* (London: Weidenfeld & Nicolson, 1983), p. 4.
11. Ridley, *Bertie*, p. 239.
12. P. Magnus, *King Edward the Seventh* (Harmondsworth: Penguin, 1967), p. 298.
13. Ridley, *Bertie*, p. 294.
14. Magnus, *King Edward the Seventh*, p. 299.
15. Nicolson, *King George V*, p. 85.
16. Ridley, *Bertie*, p. 304.
17. R. Rhodes James (ed.), *'Chips': The Diaries of Sir Henry Channon* (London: Weidenfeld & Nicolson, 1967), p. 473.
18. Rose, *George V*, p. 43.
19. Nicolson, *King George V*, p. 97.

2. EDWARDIAN HEIR, 1901–1910

1. Buchan, *King's Grace*, p. 15.
2. Rose, *King George V*, p. 44.
3. Nicolson, *King George V*, pp. 114–15.
4. Ibid., p. 133.
5. Rose, *George V*, p. 66.
6. F. Prochaska, *Royal Bounty: The Making of a Welfare Monarchy* (New Haven, CT: Yale University Press, 1995), p. 172.
7. Nicolson, *King George V*, p. 93.
8. Rose, *George V*, p. 60.
9. J. Pope-Hennessy, *Queen Mary, 1867–1953* (London: George Allen & Unwin, 1959), p. 368.
10. Rose, *George V*, p. 56.
11. P. Ziegler, *King Edward VIII: The Official Biography* (London: Collins, 1990), p. 15.
12. Rose, *George V*, p. 59.
13. Ziegler, *King Edward VIII*, p. 24.
14. S. Bradford, *King George VI* (London: Weidenfeld & Nicolson, 1989), p. 29.
15. W. R. Louis, 'Introduction', in J. M. Brown and W. R. Louis (eds), *The Oxford History of the British Empire*, vol. 4, *The Twentieth Century* (Oxford: Oxford University Press, 1999), p. 2.
16. Nicolson, *King George V*, pp. 138–9.
17. Rose, *George V*, p. 71.
18. Nicolson, *King George V*, p. 153.

3. KING AND EMPEROR IN PEACE AND WAR, 1910–1918

1. Buchan, *King's Grace*, p. 26.
2. Pope-Hennessy, *Queen Mary*, p. 421.
3. Nicolson, *King George V*, p. 188.
4. Ibid., p. 193.
5. Rose, *George V*, p. 130.
6. K. O. Morgan (ed.), *Lloyd George Family Letters, 1885–1936* (Cardiff: University of Wales, 1973), pp. 158–9.
7. M. V. Brett and Viscount Esher (eds), *Journals and Letters of Reginald, Viscount Esher*, 4 vols (London: Ivor Nicholson & Watson, 1934–8), vol. 3, p. 48.
8. Rose, *George V*, p. 293.
9. Ibid., p. 101.
10. Nicolson, *King George V*, p. 206.
11. Ibid.
12. R. Jenkins, *Asquith* (London: HarperCollins, 1986), p. 235.
13. C. Bailey, *Black Diamonds: The Rise and Fall of an English Dynasty* (London: Penguin, 2008), p. 121.

14. Ziegler, *King Edward VIII*, pp. 43–4.
15. Rose, *George V*, p. 167.
16. Ibid.
17. Nicolson, *King George V*, p. 327.
18. M. Carter, *The Three Emperors: Three Cousins, Three Empires and the Road to the First World War* (London: Penguin, 2009), p. 436.
19. Nicolson, *King George V*, p. 329.
20. Ibid., p. 378.
21. G. Bocca, *The Uneasy Heads* (London: Weidenfeld & Nicolson, 1959), p. 170.
22. J. Gore, *King George V: A Personal Memoir* (London: John Murray, 1949), p. 175.

4. REVOLUTION AND COUNTER-REVOLUTION, 1918–1929

1. Buchan, *King's Grace*, pp. 113–14.
2. S. Roskill, *Hankey: Man of Secrets*, 3 vols (London: Collins, 1970–74), vol. 2, p. 28.
3. Earl of Oxford and Asquith, *H. H. A., Letters of the Earl of Oxford and Asquith to a Friend*, 2 vols (London: Geoffrey Bles, 1933–4), vol. 1, p. 30.
4. Rose, *George V*, p. 229.
5. F. M. L. Thompson, *English Landed Society in the Nineteenth Century* (London: Routledge & Kegan Paul, 1963), p. 330.
6. C. Cross (ed.), *Life with Lloyd George: The Diary of A. J. Sylvester, 1931–45* (London: Macmillan, 1975), pp. 93–4.
7. Nicolson, *King George V*, p. 460.
8. Ibid., p. 470.
9. Rose, *George V*, p. 242.
10. Prochaska, *Royal Bounty*, p. 182.
11. J. W. Wheeler-Bennett, *King George VI: His Life and Reign* (London: Macmillan, 1958), pp. 159–60.
12. Prochaska, *Royal Bounty*, pp. 183–4.
13. Ibid., p. 186.
14. P. Hall, *Royal Fortune: Tax, Money and the Monarchy* (London: Bloomsbury, 1992), p. 41.
15. Rose, *George V*, pp. 312, 318.
16. Ziegler, *King Edward VIII*, p. 111.
17. Pope-Hennessy, *Queen Mary*, p. 520.
18. Ziegler, *King Edward VIII*, p. 114.
19. Nicolson, *King George V*, p. 497.
20. Ibid., p. 520.
21. Rose, *George V*, p. 340.
22. Nicolson, *King George V*, p. 542.
23. J. Barnes and D. Nicholson (eds), *The Leo Amery Diaries*, 2 vols (London: Hutchinson, 1980–88), vol. 1, p. 536.
24. W. Shawcross (ed.), *Counting One's Blessings: The Selected Letters of Queen Elizabeth the Queen Mother* (London: Macmillan, 2012), p. 127.
25. Rose, *George V*, p. 322.

26. Ibid., p. 288.
27. Pope-Hennessy, *Queen Mary*, p. 548.
28. Rose, *George V*, p. 357.

5. DEPRESSION AND JUBILATION, 1929–1936

1. Buchan, *King's Grace*, p. 156.
2. Nicolson, *King George V*, p. 577.
3. Rose, *King George V*, p. 374.
4. Ibid., p. 382.
5. Ibid., pp. 387–8.
6. A. J. P. Taylor (ed.), *Frances Stevenson: Lloyd George: A Diary* (London: Hutchinson, 1971), p. 309.
7. Viscount Templewood, *Nine Troubled Years* (London: Collins, 1954), p. 159.
8. Nicolson, *King George V*, p. 604.
9. Rose, *George V*, p. 348.
10. Templewood, *Nine Troubled Years*, pp. 59–60.
11. Nicolson, *King George V*, p. 650.
12. Ibid., p. 606.
13. Rose, *George V*, p. 394.
14. Nicolson, *King George V*, pp. 670–71.
15. Shawcross (ed.), *Counting One's Blessings*, p. 200.
16. Rose, *George V*, p. 392.
17. Mabell, Countess of Airlie, *Thatched with Gold* (London: Hutchinson, 1962), p. 197.
18. Nicolson, *King George V*, p. 669.
19. Ibid., p. 670.
20. D. Cannadine, *G. M. Trevelyan: A Life in History* (New York: Norton, 1993), p. 238.
21. Prochaska, *Royal Bounty*, p. 208.
22. Rose, *George V*, p. 395.
23. Ibid., p. 398.
24. K. Middlemas and J. Barnes, *Baldwin: A Biography* (London: Weidenfeld & Nicolson, 1969), p. 976.
25. Rose, *George V*, p. 389.
26. Ibid., p. 402.
27. Ibid., p. 360.
28. S. Baldwin, *Service of Our Lives: Last Speeches as Prime Minister* (London: Hodder & Stoughton, 1938), p. 28.
29. Pope-Hennessy, *Queen Mary*, p. 559.
30. R. C. Self (ed.), *The Austen Chamberlain Diary Letters: The Correspondence of Sir Austen Chamberlain with His Sisters Hilda and Ida, 1916–1937* (Cambridge: Cambridge University Press, 1995), p. 498.
31. N. Nicolson (ed.), *Harold Nicolson: Diaries and Letters, 1945–62* (London: Collins, 1968), p. 241.
32. Self (ed.), *Austen Chamberlain Diary Letters*, p. 498.

Further Reading

Among recent British monarchs, King George V has received extensive, indeed outstanding, biographical treatment. For an interim account, to mark George V's Silver Jubilee, see John Buchan, *The King's Grace, 1910–1935* (London: Hodder & Stoughton, 1935). The official biography is divided into two parts: John Gore, *King George V: A Personal Memoir* (London: John Murray, 1949), deals with his private life, and Harold Nicolson, *King George V: His Life and Reign* (London: Constable, 1952), describes and analyses his performance as a constitutional monarch. Both books are finely detailed, yet also reticent and respectful, tactful and urbane. Two more recent biographies, Denis Judd, *The Life and Times of George V* (London: Weidenfeld & Nicolson, 1973), and Kenneth Rose, *King George V* (London: Weidenfeld & Nicolson, 1983), deal more candidly with the monarch's whole life, soberly in the case of Judd, scintillatingly in the case of Rose; and there is an exemplary brief life by H. C. G. Matthew, 'George V (1865–1936)', *Oxford Dictionary of National Biography* (Oxford: Oxford University Press, 2004), online edition http://www.oxforddnb.com/view/article/33369. Queen Mary has also been fully treated in James Pope-Hennessy, *Queen Mary, 1867–1953* (London: George Allen & Unwin, 1959), and Anne Edwards, *Matriarch: Queen Mary and the House of Windsor* (New York: William Morrow, 1984). There are also many references to the king and queen in the published diaries from the time, some of which are cited in the Notes.

The forebears, progeny and relatives of King George V have also received very thorough biographical attention. For his grandmother, see Elizabeth Longford, *Victoria R.I.* (London: Weidenfeld &

Nicolson, 1964), which remains unsurpassed, fifty years after it first appeared. For the king's father, there is Sir Sidney Lee, *King Edward VII: A Biography*, 2 vols (London: Macmillan, 1925–7); Philip Magnus, *King Edward the Seventh* (Harmondsworth: Penguin, 1967); and Jane Ridley, *Bertie: A Life of Edward VII* (London: Chatto & Windus, 2012), which is much the best; for his mother, see Georgina Battiscombe, *Queen Alexandra* (London: Cardinal Books, 1969). For his eldest son, see Frances Donaldson, *Edward VIII* (London: Weidenfeld & Nicolson, 1974), and Philip Ziegler, *King Edward VIII: The Official Biography* (London: Collins, 1990); both are excellent. For George V's second son, there is John W. Wheeler-Bennett's very courtly *King George VI: His Life and Reign* (London: Macmillan, 1958), and Sarah Bradford's more critical *King George VI* (London: Weidenfeld & Nicolson, 1989); for his favourite daughter-in-law, see William Shawcross, *Queen Elizabeth the Queen Mother: The Official Biography* (London: Macmillan, 2009), and *idem* (ed.), *Counting One's Blessings: The Selected Letters of Queen Elizabeth the Queen Mother* (London: Macmillan, 2012).

The serious historical study of the modern British monarchy, going beyond the conventional reign-by-reign biographical treatment, and addressing broader themes and questions, is a relatively recent scholarly development. For two initial forays, see David Cannadine, 'The Context, Performance and Meaning of Ritual: The British Monarchy and the "Invention of Tradition", *c.* 1820–1977', in Eric Hobsbawm and Terence Ranger (eds), *The Invention of Tradition* (Cambridge: Cambridge University Press, 1983); and idem, 'The Last Hanoverian Sovereign? The Victorian Monarchy in Historical Perspective, 1688–1988', in A. L. Beier, D. Cannadine and J. M. Rosenheim (eds.), *The First Modern Society: Essays in English History in Honour of Lawrence Stone* (Cambridge: Cambridge University Press, 1989). A perceptive study of the monarchy and national life in George V's day is Ross McKibbin, *Classes and Cultures: England 1918–1951* (Oxford: Oxford University Press, 1998), while Andrzej Olechnowicz (ed.), *The Monarchy and the British Nation, 1780 to the Present* (Cambridge: Cambridge University Press, 2007), is a fine recent collection of essays. For particular subjects, see Vernon Bogdanor, *The Monarchy and the*

Constitution (Oxford: Clarendon Press, 1995); Philip Hall, *Royal Fortune: Tax, Money and the Monarchy* (London: Bloomsbury, 1992); Frank Prochaska, *Royal Bounty: The Making of a Welfare Monarchy* (New Haven, CT: Yale University Press, 1995); and James Loughlin, *The British Monarchy and Ireland, 1800 to the Present* (Cambridge: Cambridge University Press, 2007).

Picture Credits

(Images 1–4 © Getty Images, 5–12 © Bridgeman Art)

Acknowledgements

When Harold Nicolson agreed to write the official life of King George V in the summer of 1948, he thought it would 'provide interesting work and give me an excuse for doing nothing else', and when he began the first chapter, he likened his task to 'starting in a taxi [from London] on the way to Vladivostok'. Over half a century later, I have found writing this short biography no less interesting, and the cab ride has been nothing like as lengthy. But I have accumulated many debts along the way, which it is a pleasure to acknowledge here. My first thanks go to Simon Winder, my long-time editor and friend at the Penguin Press, who asked me to write this book, and who has provided advice and support throughout, to Kate Parker, who has carefully and meticulously copy-edited my text, and to Anna Hervé, who has seen the book through to publication with exemplary conscientiousness and care. I am deeply grateful to the historians and biographers who, in the decades since Nicolson, have significantly enhanced our understanding of the modern British monarchy, and on whose work I have extensively and appreciatively drawn. I am equally beholden to many former students at Cambridge and Columbia Universities, where I taught courses on the modern British monarchy during the 1980s and 1990s, and from whom I learned a great deal. I owe a particular debt to the late Eric Hobsbawm, the late J. H. Plumb and to Keith Thomas, who first encouraged me to work on sovereigns and spectacle, and also to Merlin Waterson for one crucial reference. And I again offer up my loving thanks to Linda Colley, for having read and commented on an earlier draft of this book, and for so much more besides. In the interests of full disclosure, I must also record that, by agreeable coincidence, I have written this book in the English county that King George V loved the

ACKNOWLEDGEMENTS

most; but so far as I am aware, this is, beyond my abiding historical curiosity about him, the only significant connection between subject and author.

David Cannadine
Norfolk
August 2013

Index

Penguin Monarchs

THE HOUSES OF WESSEX AND DENMARK

THE HOUSES OF NORMANDY, BLOIS AND ANJOU

THE HOUSE OF PLANTAGENET

THE HOUSES OF LANCASTER AND YORK

* Now in paperback

THE HOUSE OF TUDOR

Henry VII	Sean Cunningham
Henry VIII*	John Guy
Edward VI*	Stephen Alford
Mary I*	John Edwards
Elizabeth I	Helen Castor

THE HOUSE OF STUART

James I	Thomas Cogswell
Charles I*	Mark Kishlansky
[Cromwell*	David Horspool]
Charles II*	Clare Jackson
James II	David Womersley
William III & Mary II*	Jonathan Keates
Anne	Richard Hewlings

THE HOUSE OF HANOVER

George I	Tim Blanning
George II	Norman Davies
George III	Amanda Foreman
George IV	Stella Tillyard
William IV	Roger Knight
Victoria*	Jane Ridley

THE HOUSES OF SAXE-COBURG & GOTHA AND WINDSOR

Edward VII*	Richard Davenport-Hines
George V*	David Cannadine
Edward VIII*	Piers Brendon
George VI*	Philip Ziegler
Elizabeth II*	Douglas Hurd

* Now in paperback

ALLEN LANE
an imprint of
PENGUIN BOOKS

Also Published

Stephen Kotkin, *Stalin, Vol. II: Waiting for Hitler, 1928-1941*

Lindsey Fitzharris, *The Butchering Art: Joseph Lister's Quest to Transform the Grisly World of Victorian Medicine*

Serhii Plokhy, *Lost Kingdom: A History of Russian Nationalism from Ivan the Great to Vladimir Putin*

Mark Mazower, *What You Did Not Tell: A Russian Past and the Journey Home*

Lawrence Freedman, *The Future of War: A History*

Niall Ferguson, *The Square and the Tower: Networks, Hierarchies and the Struggle for Global Power*

Matthew Walker, *Why We Sleep: The New Science of Sleep and Dreams*

Edward O. Wilson, *The Origins of Creativity*

John Bradshaw, *The Animals Among Us: The New Science of Anthropology*

David Cannadine, *Victorious Century: The United Kingdom, 1800-1906*

Leonard Susskind and Art Friedman, *Special Relativity and Classical Field Theory*

Maria Alyokhina, *Riot Days*

Oona A. Hathaway and Scott J. Shapiro, *The Internationalists: And Their Plan to Outlaw War*

Chris Renwick, *Bread for All: The Origins of the Welfare State*

Anne Applebaum, *Red Famine: Stalin's War on Ukraine*

Richard McGregor, *Asia's Reckoning: The Struggle for Global Dominance*

Chris Kraus, *After Kathy Acker: A Biography*

Clair Wills, *Lovers and Strangers: An Immigrant History of Post-War Britain*

Odd Arne Westad, *The Cold War: A World History*

Max Tegmark, *Life 3.0: Being Human in the Age of Artificial Intelligence*

Jonathan Losos, *Improbable Destinies: How Predictable is Evolution?*

Chris D. Thomas, *Inheritors of the Earth: How Nature Is Thriving in an Age of Extinction*

Chris Patten, *First Confession: A Sort of Memoir*

James Delbourgo, *Collecting the World: The Life and Curiosity of Hans Sloane*

Naomi Klein, *No Is Not Enough: Defeating the New Shock Politics*

Ulrich Raulff, *Farewell to the Horse: The Final Century of Our Relationship*

Slavoj Žižek, *The Courage of Hopelessness: Chronicles of a Year of Acting Dangerously*

Patricia Lockwood, *Priestdaddy: A Memoir*

Ian Johnson, *The Souls of China: The Return of Religion After Mao*

Stephen Alford, *London's Triumph: Merchant Adventurers and the Tudor City*

Hugo Mercier and Dan Sperber, *The Enigma of Reason: A New Theory of Human Understanding*

Stuart Hall, *Familiar Stranger: A Life Between Two Islands*

Allen Ginsberg, *The Best Minds of My Generation: A Literary History of the Beats*

Sayeeda Warsi, *The Enemy Within: A Tale of Muslim Britain*

Alexander Betts and Paul Collier, *Refuge: Transforming a Broken Refugee System*

Robert Bickers, *Out of China: How the Chinese Ended the Era of Western Domination*

Erica Benner, *Be Like the Fox: Machiavelli's Lifelong Quest for Freedom*

William D. Cohan, *Why Wall Street Matters*

David Horspool, *Oliver Cromwell: The Protector*

Daniel C. Dennett, *From Bacteria to Bach and Back: The Evolution of Minds*

Derek Thompson, *Hit Makers: How Things Become Popular*

Harriet Harman, *A Woman's Work*

Wendell Berry, *The World-Ending Fire: The Essential Wendell Berry*

Daniel Levin, *Nothing but a Circus: Misadventures among the Powerful*

Stephen Church, *Henry III: A Simple and God-Fearing King*

Pankaj Mishra, *Age of Anger: A History of the Present*

Graeme Wood, *The Way of the Strangers: Encounters with the Islamic State*

Michael Lewis, *The Undoing Project: A Friendship that Changed the World*

John Romer, *A History of Ancient Egypt, Volume 2: From the Great Pyramid to the Fall of the Middle Kingdom*

Andy King, *Edward I: A New King Arthur?*

Thomas L. Friedman, *Thank You for Being Late: An Optimist's Guide to Thriving in the Age of Accelerations*

John Edwards, *Mary I: The Daughter of Time*

Grayson Perry, *The Descent of Man*

Deyan Sudjic, *The Language of Cities*

Norman Ohler, *Blitzed: Drugs in Nazi Germany*

Carlo Rovelli, *Reality Is Not What It Seems: The Journey to Quantum Gravity*

Catherine Merridale, *Lenin on the Train*

Susan Greenfield, *A Day in the Life of the Brain: The Neuroscience of Consciousness from Dawn Till Dusk*

Christopher Given-Wilson, *Edward II: The Terrors of Kingship*

Emma Jane Kirby, *The Optician of Lampedusa*

Minoo Dinshaw, *Outlandish Knight: The Byzantine Life of Steven Runciman*

Candice Millard, *Hero of the Empire: The Making of Winston Churchill*

Christopher de Hamel, *Meetings with Remarkable Manuscripts*

Brian Cox and Jeff Forshaw, *Universal: A Guide to the Cosmos*

Ryan Avent, *The Wealth of Humans: Work and Its Absence in the Twenty-first Century*

Jodie Archer and Matthew L. Jockers, *The Bestseller Code*

Cathy O'Neil, *Weapons of Math Destruction: How Big Data Increases Inequality and Threatens Democracy*

Peter Wadhams, *A Farewell to Ice: A Report from the Arctic*

Richard J. Evans, *The Pursuit of Power: Europe, 1815-1914*

Anthony Gottlieb, *The Dream of Enlightenment: The Rise of Modern Philosophy*

Marc Morris, *William I: England's Conqueror*

Gareth Stedman Jones, *Karl Marx: Greatness and Illusion*

J.C.H. King, *Blood and Land: The Story of Native North America*

Robert Gerwarth, *The Vanquished: Why the First World War Failed to End, 1917-1923*

Joseph Stiglitz, *The Euro: And Its Threat to Europe*

John Bradshaw and Sarah Ellis, *The Trainable Cat: How to Make Life Happier for You and Your Cat*

A J Pollard, *Edward IV: The Summer King*

Erri de Luca, *The Day Before Happiness*

Diarmaid MacCulloch, *All Things Made New: Writings on the Reformation*

Daniel Beer, *The House of the Dead: Siberian Exile Under the Tsars*

Tom Holland, *Athelstan: The Making of England*

Christopher Goscha, *The Penguin History of Modern Vietnam*

Mark Singer, *Trump and Me*

Roger Scruton, *The Ring of Truth: The Wisdom of Wagner's Ring of the Nibelung*

Ruchir Sharma, *The Rise and Fall of Nations: Ten Rules of Change in the Post-Crisis World*

Jonathan Sumption, *Edward III: A Heroic Failure*

Daniel Todman, *Britain's War: Into Battle, 1937-1941*

Dacher Keltner, *The Power Paradox: How We Gain and Lose Influence*

Tom Gash, *Criminal: The Truth About Why People Do Bad Things*

Brendan Simms, *Britain's Europe: A Thousand Years of Conflict and Cooperation*

Slavoj Žižek, *Against the Double Blackmail: Refugees, Terror, and Other Troubles with the Neighbours*

Lynsey Hanley, *Respectable: The Experience of Class*

Piers Brendon, *Edward VIII: The Uncrowned King*

Matthew Desmond, *Evicted: Poverty and Profit in the American City*

T.M. Devine, *Independence or Union: Scotland's Past and Scotland's Present*

Seamus Murphy, *The Republic*

Jerry Brotton, *This Orient Isle: Elizabethan England and the Islamic World*

Srinath Raghavan, *India's War: The Making of Modern South Asia, 1939-1945*

Clare Jackson, *Charles II: The Star King*

Nandan Nilekani and Viral Shah, *Rebooting India: Realizing a Billion Aspirations*

Sunil Khilnani, *Incarnations: India in 50 Lives*

Helen Pearson, *The Life Project: The Extraordinary Story of Our Ordinary Lives*

Ben Ratliff, *Every Song Ever: Twenty Ways to Listen to Music Now*

Richard Davenport-Hines, *Edward VII: The Cosmopolitan King*

Peter H. Wilson, *The Holy Roman Empire: A Thousand Years of Europe's History*

Todd Rose, *The End of Average: How to Succeed in a World that Values Sameness*

Frank Trentmann, *Empire of Things: How We Became a World of Consumers, from the Fifteenth Century to the Twenty-First*

Laura Ashe, *Richard II: A Brittle Glory*

John Donvan and Caren Zucker, *In a Different Key: The Story of Autism*

Jack Shenker, *The Egyptians: A Radical Story*

Tim Judah, *In Wartime: Stories from Ukraine*

Serhii Plokhy, *The Gates of Europe: A History of Ukraine*

Robin Lane Fox, *Augustine: Conversions and Confessions*

Peter Hennessy and James Jinks, *The Silent Deep: The Royal Navy Submarine Service Since 1945*

Sean McMeekin, *The Ottoman Endgame: War, Revolution and the Making of the Modern Middle East, 1908–1923*

Charles Moore, *Margaret Thatcher: The Authorized Biography, Volume Two: Everything She Wants*

Dominic Sandbrook, *The Great British Dream Factory: The Strange History of Our National Imagination*

Larissa MacFarquhar, *Strangers Drowning: Voyages to the Brink of Moral Extremity*

Niall Ferguson, *Kissinger: 1923-1968: The Idealist*

Carlo Rovelli, *Seven Brief Lessons on Physics*

Tim Blanning, *Frederick the Great: King of Prussia*

Ian Kershaw, *To Hell and Back: Europe, 1914–1949*

Pedro Domingos, *The Master Algorithm: How the Quest for the Ultimate Learning Machine Will Remake Our World*

David Wootton, *The Invention of Science: A New History of the Scientific Revolution*

Hans Ulrich Obrist, *Lives of the Artists, Lives of the Architects*

Richard H. Thaler, *Misbehaving: The Making of Behavioural Economics*

Sheldon Solomon, Jeff Greenberg and Tom Pyszczynski, *Worm at the Core: On the Role of Death in Life*

Nathaniel Popper, *Digital Gold: The Untold Story of Bitcoin*

Dominic Lieven, *Towards the Flame: Empire, War and the End of Tsarist Russia*

Noel Malcolm, *Agents of Empire: Knights, Corsairs, Jesuits and Spies in the Sixteenth-Century Mediterranean World*

James Rebanks, *The Shepherd's Life: A Tale of the Lake District*

David Brooks, *The Road to Character*

Joseph Stiglitz, *The Great Divide*

Ken Robinson and Lou Aronica, *Creative Schools: Revolutionizing Education from the Ground Up*

Clotaire Rapaille and Andrés Roemer, *Move UP: Why Some Cultures Advances While Others Don't*

Jonathan Keates, *William III and Mary II: Partners in Revolution*

David Womersley, *James II: The Last Catholic King*

Richard Barber, *Henry II: A Prince Among Princes*

Jane Ridley, *Victoria: Queen, Matriarch, Empress*

John Gray, *The Soul of the Marionette: A Short Enquiry into Human Freedom*

Emily Wilson, *Seneca: A Life*

Michael Barber, *How to Run a Government: So That Citizens Benefit and Taxpayers Don't Go Crazy*

Dana Thomas, *Gods and Kings: The Rise and Fall of Alexander McQueen and John Galliano*

Steven Weinberg, *To Explain the World: The Discovery of Modern Science*

Jennifer Jacquet, *Is Shame Necessary?: New Uses for an Old Tool*

Eugene Rogan, *The Fall of the Ottomans: The Great War in the Middle East, 1914-1920*

Norman Doidge, *The Brain's Way of Healing: Stories of Remarkable Recoveries and Discoveries*

John Hooper, *The Italians*

Sven Beckert, *Empire of Cotton: A New History of Global Capitalism*

Mark Kishlansky, *Charles I: An Abbreviated Life*

Philip Ziegler, *George VI: The Dutiful King*

David Cannadine, *George V: The Unexpected King*

Stephen Alford, *Edward VI: The Last Boy King*

John Guy, *Henry VIII: The Quest for Fame*

Robert Tombs, *The English and their History: The First Thirteen Centuries*

Neil MacGregor, *Germany: The Memories of a Nation*

Uwe Tellkamp, *The Tower: A Novel*

Roberto Calasso, *Ardor*

Slavoj Žižek, *Trouble in Paradise: Communism After the End of History*

Francis Pryor, *Home: A Time Traveller's Tales from Britain's Prehistory*

R. F. Foster, *Vivid Faces: The Revolutionary Generation in Ireland, 1890-1923*

Andrew Roberts, *Napoleon the Great*

Shami Chakrabarti, *On Liberty*

Bessel van der Kolk, *The Body Keeps the Score: Mind, Brain and Body in the Transformation of Trauma*

Brendan Simms, *The Longest Afternoon: The 400 Men Who Decided the Battle of Waterloo*

Naomi Klein, *This Changes Everything: Capitalism vs the Climate*

Owen Jones, *The Establishment: And How They Get Away with It*

Caleb Scharf, *The Copernicus Complex: Our Cosmic Significance in a Universe of Planets and Probabilities*

Martin Wolf, *The Shifts and the Shocks: What We've Learned - and Have Still to Learn - from the Financial Crisis*

Steven Pinker, *The Sense of Style: The Thinking Person's Guide to Writing in the 21st Century*

Vincent Deary, *How We Are: Book One of the How to Live Trilogy*

Henry Kissinger, *World Order*

Alexander Watson, *Ring of Steel: Germany and Austria-Hungary at War, 1914-1918*

Richard Vinen, *National Service: Conscription in Britain, 1945-1963*

Paul Dolan, *Happiness by Design: Finding Pleasure and Purpose in Everyday Life*

Mark Greengrass, *Christendom Destroyed: Europe 1517-1650*

Hugh Thomas, *World Without End: The Global Empire of Philip II*

Richard Layard and David M. Clark, *Thrive: The Power of Evidence-Based Psychological Therapies*

Zelda la Grange, *Good Morning, Mr Mandela*

Ahron Bregman, *Cursed Victory: A History of Israel and the Occupied Territories*

Tristram Hunt, *Ten Cities that Made an Empire*

Jordan Ellenberg, *How Not to Be Wrong: The Power of Mathematical Thinking*

David Marquand, *Mammon's Kingdom: An Essay on Britain, Now*

Justin Marozzi, *Baghdad: City of Peace, City of Blood*

Adam Tooze, *The Deluge: The Great War and the Remaking of Global Order 1916-1931*

John Micklethwait and Adrian Wooldridge, *The Fourth Revolution: The Global Race to Reinvent the State*

Steven D. Levitt and Stephen J. Dubner, *Think Like a Freak: How to Solve Problems, Win Fights and Be a Slightly Better Person*

Alexander Monro, *The Paper Trail: An Unexpected History of the World's Greatest Invention*

Jacob Soll, *The Reckoning: Financial Accountability and the Making and Breaking of Nations*

Gerd Gigerenzer, *Risk Savvy: How to Make Good Decisions*

James Lovelock, *A Rough Ride to the Future*

Michael Lewis, *Flash Boys*

Hans Ulrich Obrist, *Ways of Curating*

Mai Jia, *Decoded: A Novel*

Richard Mabey, *Dreams of the Good Life: The Life of Flora Thompson and the Creation of Lark Rise to Candleford*

Danny Dorling, *All That Is Solid: The Great Housing Disaster*

Leonard Susskind and Art Friedman, *Quantum Mechanics: The Theoretical Minimum*

Michio Kaku, *The Future of the Mind: The Scientific Quest to Understand, Enhance and Empower the Mind*

Nicholas Epley, *Mindwise: How we Understand what others Think, Believe, Feel and Want*

Geoff Dyer, *Contest of the Century: The New Era of Competition with China*

Yaron Matras, *I Met Lucky People: The Story of the Romani Gypsies*

Larry Siedentop, *Inventing the Individual: The Origins of Western Liberalism*

Dick Swaab, *We Are Our Brains: A Neurobiography of the Brain, from the Womb to Alzheimer's*

Max Tegmark, *Our Mathematical Universe: My Quest for the Ultimate Nature of Reality*

David Pilling, *Bending Adversity: Japan and the Art of Survival*